French Units in the Waffen-SS

Rolf Michaelis

Schiffer Publishing Ltd

4880 Lower Valley Road • Atglen, PA 19310

Other Schiffer Books by the Author:
Ukrainians in the Waffen-SS (978-0-7643-3349-1)
Estonians in the Waffen-SS (978-0-7643-3350-7)
Cavalry Divisions of the Waffen-SS (978-0-7643-3661-4)
Panzergrenadier Divisions of the Waffen-SS (978-0-7643-3660-7)
The Kaminski Brigade (978-0-7643-3765-9)
Belgians in the Waffen-SS (978-0-7643-4034-5)

Translated from the German by David Johnston.
Originally published as,
Franzosen in der Waffen-SS,

Library of Congress Control Number: 2016943331

Cover design by Matt Goodman
Type set in Minion Pro
ISBN: 978-0-7643-5181-5
Printed in China

Published by Schiffer Publishing, Ltd.
4880 Lower Valley Road
Atglen, PA 19310
Phone: (610) 593-1777; Fax: (610) 593-2002
E-mail: Info@schifferbooks.com
Web: www.schifferbooks.com

Contents

Preface

Numerous publications have appeared in Germany and elsewhere about the French SS volunteers who fought on the German side on the eastern front. Most are based on the memories of former members and as a result objectivity sometimes takes a back seat.

This situation is taken into account in this book. In addition to providing the most comprehensive description of the history of the French units of the Waffen-SS possible, it also points out previously overlooked facts.

Selfless support is always welcome—also for this work, and so I wish to thank everyone who contributed to its realization. Special thanks to Thierry Burgeot and Kaja and Pawel Palasz.

In the hope of having created an objective and informative publication, I ask that the reader bear in mind that the misery that the Second World War brought with it cannot be captured in this book.

Rolf Michaelis

Berlin, August 2013

The *Französische-Freiwilligen-Grenadier-Regiment*

While Heinrich Himmler began recruiting for the SS in the so-called "Germanic" countries[1] in 1940,[2] the *Reichsführer-SS* initially ignored the French for racial-ideological reasons. In the summer of 1941, Otto Abetz, the German ambassador in Paris, proposed forming a legion—like those in Spain and Croatia, for example—of approximately 30,000 Frenchmen to fight in the "Crusade against Bolshevism." In response the German government declared that: "it is not desirable [...] politically to take such a large number of French volunteers [...] into the German armed services."

For propaganda reasons, however, on July 11, 1941, Hitler authorized the formation of a French volunteer legion ("*Légion des volontaires français contre le bolchévisme*" – LVF), which took part in the Russian campaign as *Französisches Infanterie-Regiment 638* (French Infantry Regiment 638) within the German army. This also satisfied the French paramilitary organizations, which wanted to play a role in the defeat of communism in Europe.

About a year later, Himmler reversed his position towards the French. After proposals by the head of the "Germanic Central Office" in the *SS-Hauptamt* (*SS-Sturmbannführer* Riedweg) in the summer of 1942, Himmler saw the possibility of enlarging his Waffen-SS by using "especially racially-pure, Germanic-looking" Frenchmen. Patterned on the "Germanic SS in the Netherlands," Himmler initially planned to form a French *SS-Sturmbann* within the Allgemeine-SS and soon afterwards a French *SS-Standarte*. Following discussions with *SS-Gruppenführer* Jüttner, then deputy chief of the *SS-Hauptamt*, and *SS-Obergruppenführer* Wolff, chief of the *Reichsführer-SS*' personal staff, at the Wolfsschanze on December 7, 1942, Himmler proposed the name "Gobineau."[3]

Joseph Arthur de Gobineau was born in Ville d'Avray near Paris on July 14, 1816, and later became a diplomat. He was known primarily for his theory of the Aryan master race and the harmfulness of miscegenation. Between 1853 and 1855 he wrote a four-volume work titled *An Essay on the Inequality of Human Races* (*Essai sur l'inégalité des races humaines*). In it Gobineau expressed his thoughts on the Aryan race. Among them, he believed that it was primarily found in Scandinavia and in the French aristocracy. He viewed Germany as a cultural mixture of the Slavs and Celts. Despite these views, his thinking represented an important pillar in Hitler's later thoughts and actions. He died in Turin on October 13, 1882.

On December 10, 1942, Himmler gave a speech in Hitler's presence in which he addressed the reorganization of the Waffen-SS and the police. He also spoke about a French SS legion and the recruitment of volunteers for it. Two days later, in a follow-up to recent discussions, in a letter to the "Führer" Himmler proposed the already-planned name *Gobineau* for a *Standarte* of the Allgemeine-SS and *Karl der Grosse* (*Charlemagne*) for a French volunteer unit of the Waffen-SS.[4] Internally, however, Himmler was already planning the formation of an SS volunteer division through a homogeneous gathering of all right-wing French paramilitary units by means of a Waffen-SS replacement command. After Hitler gave his blessing, Otto Abetz, the German ambassador in Paris, held discussions with the Vichy government. The purpose of these talks was to create the legal foundations for the French SS legion. Interestingly, *SS-Gruppenführer* Oberg, senior SS and police commander in the area of the military commander in France, was very skeptical about Himmler's suggestions. He warned that: "while on the surface a policy of cooperation is to be followed in accordance with the *Führer*'s directive, we must never lose sight of the goal of the ultimate destruction of France. The formation of an Allgemeine-SS or other similar integrated national French organization with the help of the SS would, however, provide the basis for a real national rebuilding of France, which would be contrary to the Führer's directive. If such a united organization were created, we would lose the ability to play off the various political directions in France, including the Darnand militia, against each other."[5]

And so a general centralization of all French paramilitary formations into a unit of the Allgemeine-SS did not take place. These collaborators did, however, begin recruiting for entry into a volunteer unit of the Waffen-SS.

As in many democratic countries, in France there were many small and large organizations with goals similar to those of National Socialism or fascism. They were fundamentally opposed to parliamentarianism and wished for an authoritarian national leadership, with emphasis on the struggle against bolshevism, Marxism and usually also "Jewish" capitalism. Nevertheless they differed from one another on various points, so that alliances between them were—if at all—short lived and there was never an influential, quantitatively strong concentration.[6]

Among these right-leaning movements was the *Action Française* formed in 1898. It wanted the return of the monarchy, and Duc de Guise, the Bourbon pretender to the throne, was to become head of state as Jean III. The following oath was introduced for members of the group:

> French by birth, heart, reason and will, I shall fulfill the duties of a conscious patriot. I pledge myself to fight against every republican regime. The republican spirit disorganizes national defense and favors religious influences directly hostile to traditional Catholicism. A regime that is French must be restored to France. Our only future lies, therefore, in the Monarch, as it is personified in the heir of the forty kings who, for a thousand years, made France. Only the Monarchy ensures public safety and, in its responsibility for order.

Although a supporter of traditional Catholicism, *Action Française* was ostracized by the Vatican for openly promulgating pagan ideas. Formed in 1910, the *Commissaires d'Áction Française* represented the marching wing of the movement. With about 70,000 members out a population of forty-two million, *Action Française* was not a particularly influential organization, however.

Founded in 1924, under the leadership of Pierre Taittinger, the *Jeunesses Patriotes* (Patriotic Youths) had about 85,000 members. Its political objective differed from the "monarcho-fascism" of *Action Française* primarily in its acceptance of the Republican state. The *Troupe de choc* (Storm Troop) engaged in numerous street brawls against socialist and communist organizations from 1925 and it introduced a uniform, which included the typical Basque cap. This was later copied by many right-wing organizations. The *Jeunesses Patriotes* was banned by the French government in June 1936, but it remained active under various names until 1944. It joined forces with *Solidarité Française* to form the *Front Nationale* (National Front). Of its twenty-four leading functionaries, fifteen became members of the Vichy government.

The strongest nationalist movement in France was the *Croix de Feu* (Cross of Fire) established in 1927, which reached a peak membership of 700,000. Its leader was Col. Robert de la Rocque, who once declared:

> Because we have not tied ourselves to any political party or combination, because we, exposing the collapse of the political parties, are not subject to any party influence, the nation expects of us truth, counsel and salvation. We must not disappoint the expectations of the motherland. I have no other

ambition but to serve, without any personal hidden agenda and without shrinking before any patriotic task, or any social postulate.

The support the *Croix de Feu* received stemmed from the fact that it placed patriotism above all else. Polemical hostilities were secondary. Members undoubtedly volunteered for the LVF—volunteers for the Waffen-SS, however, were marginal.

In addition, in 1933, Henry Coston founded the *Parti Socialiste National de France* (National Socialist Party of France). From July 1934, it was led by Pierre Clementi and was briefly called the *Parti Français National-Communiste.* The public's basic disinterest in the party's objectives, which included the general expulsion of the Jews and confiscation of their property for the benefit of the French nation, was reflected in the fact that it had only about 2,000 members. In late 1934, under Maurice-Christian Dubernard, the movement's name was changed back to *Parti Socialiste National de France.*

Founded at the beginning of the 1930s by François Coty, *Solidarité Française* (French Solidarity) had similar goals, which were summed up in its slogan "France for the French." Its objectives were similar to those of the NSDAP and with about 90,000 followers it was the third-strongest nationalist movement in France. On May 7, 1934, the *Solidarité Française* joined with the *Jeunesses Patriotes* to form the *Front National* (National Front). About 175,000 French nationalists were thus combined in a single organization.

Approximately 35,000 Frenchmen belonged to the *Le Francisme* (Francist) movement, which was established in Paris by Marcel Bucard on September 29, 1933. In contrast to *Solidarité Française*, *Le Francisme* gravitated, not towards German National Socialism, but towards Italian fascism. It was thus more liberal towards the Jews than was the case with French Solidarity. In 1938, Bucard tried to establish the *Parti Franciste* (Francist Party) from his *Mouvement franciste*, which had financial backing from Italy. In fact, however, it did not gain a certain degree of importance until after the defeat of France in the summer of 1940—this time with financial support from the Vichy government. Membership numbers were below 8,000, nevertheless the youth wing of the party, the *Jeunesse franciste* (French Youth) represented a not insignificant part of the volunteers of the LVF and the French *SS-Freiwilligen-Sturmbrigade* (SS Volunteer Assault Brigade). In Bucard's eyes, his francist movement was a French form of Italian fascism. In the beginning its attitude towards the Jewish population was almost liberal, but as the war went on this changed, until Bucard became a committed anti-Semite.

Aimé-Joseph Darnand, leader of the French Militia.

Surprisingly, despite its name the *Milice Socialiste Nationale* (National Socialist Militia) rejected anti-Semitism, however, it was against freemasonry and the parliamentary system. The party's program also included a close and amicable relationship with Germany. With only about 2,000 members, however, this movement under Gustave Hervé was of no political significance.

In July 1936, Jacques Doriot, a former communist, founded the *Parti Populaire Française* (French People's Party). Many workers but also conservative nationalists joined its ranks. Still relatively liberal in the beginning, Doriot turned not only to the capital, but also to Italian fascism, which also supported him. By 1937, the party already had about 200,000 members. After the military defeat of France in the summer of 1940, Doriot increasingly gained importance and in 1941, together with Marcel Déat, leader of the *Rassemblement National Populaire*, and Eugéne Deloncle, leader of the *Mouvement social révolutionnaire*, became major supporters of the LVF. One year later, during preliminary discussions relating to the formation of a French SS legion, Doriot declared that he could provide about 600 volunteers from his movement alone, which included the *Jeunesses Populaires Français* (French People's Youth) as its youth organization.

The *Rassemblement National Populaire* (National People's Assembly) was founded by Marcel Déat in March 1941. Like the *Parti Populaire Française* this fascist movement included former socialists and communists in its ranks. In contrast to Doriot, Déat's goal was an authoritarian republic. Interestingly, of the about 25,000 members, a not inconsiderable part of the youth group belonged to the French People's Party (*Parti Populaire Française*). The party's military wing was called the *Legion nationale populaire* (National People's Legion), which in 1943 was renamed the *Milice nationale populaire* (National People's Militia).

In June 1940, after the defeat of France and the start of the German occupation, Eugene Deloncle formed the *Mouvement social révolutionnaire* (Social Revolutionary Movement). In doing so Deloncle supported the Vichy regime of Marshal Pétain. He was later also active in Marcel Déat's *Rassemblement national populaire* (National People's Assembly), and later there were frequent disputes between him and Déat. Déat planned to disband the social-revolutionary movement and for his part Deloncle wanted to become the sole leader of the National People's Assembly. As a result Déat ordered Deloncle dismissed from all party offices and his expulsion from the *Rassemblement national populaire*. Deloncle's dismissal resulted in the organization losing its influence in the Vichy government, however. Deloncle died on January 17, 1944, in an exchange of gunfire with the Gestapo in Paris.

Beginning in 1940, not a few members of the above-named parties and organizations volunteered to serve in the Kriegsmarine, the NSKK (National Socialist Motor Vehicle Corps), the *Légion des volontaires français contre le bolchévisme* (LVF) or the military veterans organization *Légion française des combatants* (French Legion of Combatants) from which Aimé-Joseph Darnand initially formed the *Service d'ordre légionaire* (Legionary Service Order) and finally on December 19, 1942, the *Milice Française* (French Militia). This consisted of about 30,000 militiamen, and in cooperation with the German security police it was active against political opponents in France. In January 1943, Darnand became state secretary for security and public order in France in the Vichy government. Until the summer of 1943, French Prime Minister Laval refused Darnand's request to arm the *Milice Française*. A change was finally brought about when the Germans requested that an appeal be made for members of the militia to join the Waffen-SS. In return Laval was supposed to agree to arm this formation.

Darnand himself joined the Waffen-SS as an *SS-Obersturmführer* in August 1943. Surprisingly, however, he did not join the *Französische SS-Freiwilligen-Regiment* (French SS Volunteer Regiment), but instead the *5. SS-Freiwilligen-Sturmbrigade "Wallonien"* (5th SS Assault Brigade). In a letter to *SS-Obergruppenführer* Frank, the German secretary of state for Bohemia and Moravia, *SS-Gruppenführer* von Pückler, the Waffen-SS commander-in-chief in Bohemia-Moravia, noted: "Within the French émigrés, Doriot, the leader of the Parti populaire, has won out against the direction of Darnand. Darnand has joined the Wallonian division as a volunteer."

Doriot's "winning out" against Darnand was the result of the power struggle between the two and the resulting position toward Germany. While the *Parti populaire* provided volunteers for the eastern front but did not actively participate in combat in France, the militia, together with the French police, also took part in inglorious activities associated with the persecution of the Jews in France. The militia also did not use kid gloves when dealing with suspected members of the *Résistance*. Like the other collaborationist organizations, the militia was disbanded by the new provisional government of de Gaulle on August 9, 1944.

After German-French negotiations on the political and military levels held out the prospect of the formation of a French SS volunteer unit, Hitler ordered the official recruiting of French volunteers for the Waffen-SS to begin. The *SS-Führungshauptamt* documented this on March 3, 1943, however after no official legal basis for this was reached with the Vichy government

A recruiting poster: "Shoulder to shoulder against the common enemy! French division of the Waffen-SS."

The recruiting office for French volunteers of the Waffen-SS at 24 Avenue du Recteur-Poincare, Paris.

and as there was uncertainty as to how many volunteers could be expected, organizationally the first men were not registered for a French SS unit but instead for the—likewise French-speaking—Wallonian Legion (effective May 1943: *5. SS-Freiwilligen-Sturmbrigade "Wallonien"*). The later *Waffen-Junker* André Bayle remembered:

> It was ten o'clock in the morning on Monday, the 15th of March 1943, when I took the decisive step, which meant walking into the rooms of the *Ersatzkommando Frankreich der Waffen-SS* in Paris, 24, avenue Recteur-Poincaré, with the firm intention of joining this elite unit of the European Waffen-SS as a volunteer ...[7]
>
> We signed service contracts for the duration of the war, then a second beginning in Sennheim in early August 1943, in order to conform with the decree of July 22, 1943 by the lawful Vichy government ...
>
> The registry office in Paris had registered us as Walloons, even though they were not yet in the Waffen-SS. This didn't happen until July 1, 1943, when the Wallonian Legion was renamed the SS Volunteer Brigade Wallonia ...[8]
>
> After a short meal break we were sent to the Clignancourt barracks, where we were to spend two days before being sent east to Germany.

As mentioned in the recollections, Prime Minister Paul Laval of the French Vichy government did not pass a law allowing French citizens to join the Waffen-SS until July 22, 1943:

> Following examination of founding acts 12 and 12a, and after agreement by the cabinet council, the head of government decrees the following:
>
> Article 1: The French are allowed to enroll voluntarily in French units formed by the German government (Waffen-SS) for the purpose of fighting bolshevism outside of France.
>
> Article 2: The members of this unit who actually fight outside state territory shall be entitled to all the benefits promised to the Legion des voluntaries français contre le bolchévisme.
>
> Article 3: This law shall be published in the Journal Officiel (official journal) and be enforced as state law.

Robert Soulat. After the war he wrote a history of the division in which he served.

"If you want France to live, fight bolshevism in the Waffen-SS."

Propaganda such as this suggested that the volunteers would be equipped with tanks and heavy weapons. This was a false assumption, as events in Pomerania were to show.

The new law was revealed to the French and foreign press on August 6, 1943:

> By enacting the law of June 22, 1943, Prime Minister Laval, in agreement with State President Marshall Pétain, has acknowledged the right of all Frenchmen to join the ranks of the Waffen-SS in the east in order to take part there in the struggle for the existence and future of Europe.
>
> Legally the Waffen-SS volunteers have the same legal status as members of the French Volunteer Legion. The French government has thus shown that it appreciates the Führer's offer and that it is ready to assume its share of the responsibilities that the decisive hours for the fate of Europe demand. It is obvious that the formation of a unit of French volunteers represents a new step towards the unification of European youth against bolshevism-nihilism.
>
> There is undoubtedly an influx of volunteers from almost every country in Europe. They want to fight side by side with their German comrades and through their boldness and bravery distinguish themselves on the Eastern Front. But they are also changing the Waffen-SS, which was essentially part of the NSDAP and originally had only a purely German significance, in that it is fusing into an inseparable community with the youth of Europe, which is now fighting for the survival of the cultural values of Europe and its civilization.
>
> The fact that more than 1,500 volunteers have come forward in a few days without any propaganda is proof that the youth of France has instinctively understood the importance of this new step. The first two battalions are already standing and soon the first regiment of the French Waffen-SS will provide proof of the great French military tradition and the fighting spirit of youth. It will do the Waffen-SS honor to take on as an important obligation the task of employing the soldierly abilities and will to fight of every Frenchman who is prepared to sacrifice his life for the existence and future of Europe in the struggle against bolshevism for social justice and victory.

One week later—on August 14, 1943—the French newspapers used this press release as an opportunity to announce the new law:

> A French regiment of the Waffen-SS has now been formed as part of the struggle of European youth against the world enemy of bolshevism.

> The age limit for volunteers is seventeen to forty, minimum height is 1.65 meters. Volunteers for the Waffen-SS are relieved of their labor obligation. French officers and non-commissioned officers retain their ranks and the non-commissioned officer and officer path is open to every volunteer from the enlisted ranks based on performance and ability. The welfare and provision of family members is governed by existing regulations. Although they are not providers, unmarried volunteers will receive an allowance that will be paid to an account that they can access in France.
>
> The first enthusiastic intakes of volunteers have shown that a significant part of the French youth has realized that the fighting youth of Germany views them as friends and comrades.

Approximately 5,000 men subsequently volunteered and they were initially assembled in the SS training camp in Sennheim (Alsace).[9] In addition to members of the previously mentioned right-wing organizations, they included volunteers already in German service (in the NSKK for example), but also adventurers and some criminals. Roughly 50% were rejected during physical examinations. This could have been for medical reasons (for example, bad teeth), physiological causes (volunteers who did not meet the "especially racially-pure, Germanic-looking" requirement) or political or moral reasons (criminality, for example).

Heinrich Wolf, a former member of the *12. SS-Panzer-Division "Hitlerjugend,"* met a former German officer who had taken part in these physical examinations in the Heilbronn POW camp in 1945:

> I met some interesting people in the medical camp. One was an *SS-Obersturmführer* and *Oberleutnant der Waffen-SS* (according to his pay book, which he showed me). This man could not be moved to the Kornwestheim camp, probably because of terrible boils. The lack of and poor quality of food effected people differently: some got phlegmon, some boils.
>
> This officer told me that he had been present when the French SS volunteers were taken in. I replied to him that by taking in so many foreigners our force had been more or less degraded into a foreign legion. The *Obersturmführer* disagreed vehemently with this objection. A judicial record was first required of every volunteer and a visual inspection was also carried out to eliminate from the beginning those

Just before their first action in Galicia, the French SS volunteers received a nationality shield with the French national colors blue-white-red. It was supposed to be worn on the tunic on the left forearm.

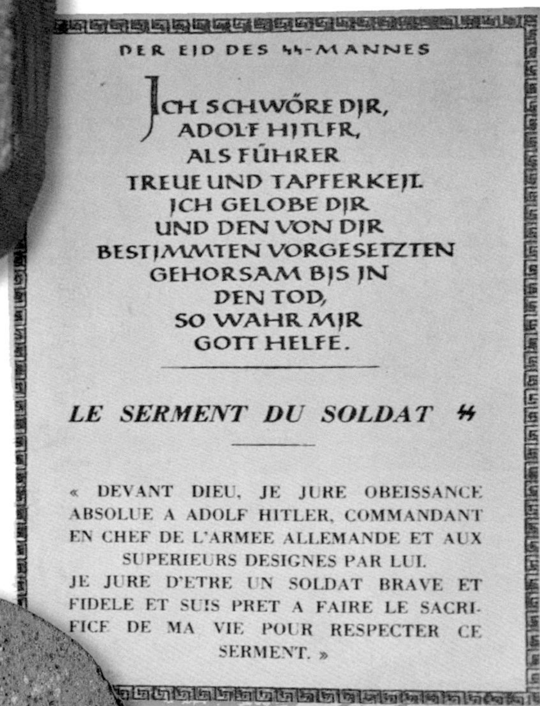

DER EID DES SS-MANNES

ICH SCHWÖRE DIR,
ADOLF HITLER,
ALS FÜHRER
TREUE UND TAPFERKEIT.
ICH GELOBE DIR
UND DEN VON DIR
BESTIMMTEN VORGESETZTEN
GEHORSAM BIS IN
DEN TOD,
SO WAHR MIR
GOTT HELFE.

LE SERMENT DU SOLDAT SS

« DEVANT DIEU, JE JURE OBEISSANCE ABSOLUE A ADOLF HITLER, COMMANDANT EN CHEF DE L'ARMEE ALLEMANDE ET AUX SUPERIEURS DESIGNES PAR LUI.
JE JURE D'ETRE UN SOLDAT BRAVE ET FIDELE ET SUIS PRET A FAIRE LE SACRIFICE DE MA VIE POUR RESPECTER CE SERMENT. »

The Waffen-SS oath in German and French: "I pledge to you, Adolf Hitler, bravery and loyalty. I pledge to you and to the superiors that you set for me obedience unto death, so help me God."

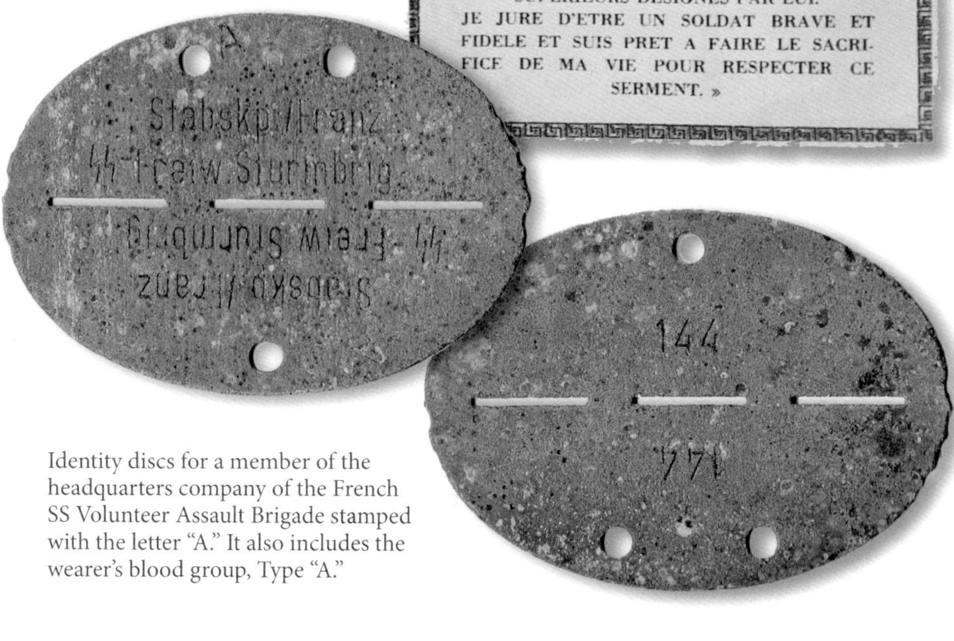

Identity discs for a member of the headquarters company of the French SS Volunteer Assault Brigade stamped with the letter "A." It also includes the wearer's blood group, Type "A."

> who appeared to be adventurers or otherwise made an unfavorable impression. As a result, only about every second one who had volunteered to fight on the Eastern Front was accepted. But these were then "idealists" and "fine lads."

After the number of volunteers in March-April fell well below what was desired, from then on press reports spoke only of a French SS volunteer regiment. The *SS-Führungshauptamt*, however, first noted this on September 18, 1943: "The Führer has ordered the formation of a French SS volunteer grenadier regiment. The planned formation of a French SS volunteer division has been set aside for the time being."

The authorized strength for a grenadier regiment envisaged three battalions with roughly the following strengths:

Officers	NCOs	Enlisted Men	Total
42	311	1,628	1,981
2.11%	15.65%	82.24%	100%

After approximately 2,700 French SS volunteers had been recruited, however, the planned number of officers was amended to about sixty and that for NCOs to about 440. The *SS-Hauptamt* issued an order on October 15, 1943, in an attempt to recruit ninety former French officers and 300 veteran NCOs for the Waffen-SS in order meet this large requirement. This was largely ineffective, for only about twenty-five volunteers took part in the "first special course for French officers at the SS-Junkersschule Tölz" from January 10 to March 11, 1944.

At the same time about sixty French SS volunteers were sent to the SS non-commissioned officer school in Posen for an eight-week course. Having completed a non-commissioned officer candidate course in Sennheim, they were now to be trained as NCOs. While the candidates were, as a rule, young men, the officers and officer candidates were mostly older members of the militia.

In spring 1944, the *SS-Führungshauptamt* designed a program in which heavy SS artillery battalions would be formed as supporting corps units. During this planning the idea was put forward of forming the ***schwere französische SS-Freiwilligen-Artillerie-Regiment (mot.) 500*** (500th Heavy French SS Volunteer Motorized Artillery Regiment) instead of the French SS Grenadier Regiment.[9]

Elements of the new regiment were sent to *SS-Artillerie-Schule II* in Beneschau and to the *SS-Artillerie-Ausbildungs- und Ersatz-Regiment* (SS Artillery Training and Replacement Regiment) in Proschitz. Following completion of the NCO course in Posen, André Bayle was ordered straight to Beneschau. He remembered the disappointment felt by the men when they learned that they were to be trained as artillerymen:

> On our arrival in Beneschau we found fantastic barracks which housed the artillery school. The next morning we were issued brand-new equipment. Our shoulder straps now had the vermillion-red braid of the artillery instead of the white of the infantry …
>
> The equipment envisaged for the French regiment was then shown to us. It was magnificent, brand-new from the factory and consisted mainly of halftracks and 105- and 150 mm howitzers. The SS officers declared that they were proud to receive French artillerymen.
>
> We carried out our first exercises in the snow and cold without much enthusiasm. In fact, our disappointment was too great …
>
> This quite disturbed the training until the blessed day when the commander of the school announced our departure for a French assault brigade.
>
> We jumped for joy …

In fact, the idea of forming five heavy SS artillery battalions and a French heavy artillery regiment as corps units was quickly abandoned. The German armaments industry was already having difficulty bringing the existing artillery units of the Wehrmacht and Waffen-SS to something approaching authorized strength after the heavy losses of the winter of 1943–44. Consequently, an *SS-Sturmbrigade "neuer Art"* (SS assault brigade "new type") was formed effective March 30, 1944.

French SS volunteers in October 1943. There is no mistaking their enthusiasm for Hitler.

Joseph Darnand (right) seeing off French SS volunteers at Paris East Station in January 1944.

The *Französische SS-Freiwilligen-Sturmbrigade*

The approximately 1,700 Frenchmen already at the Böhmen (Bohemia) training camp were transferred from the artillery replacement unit to the *SS-Panzer Grenadier-Schule* in Neweklau. There they were to form an *SS-Freiwilligen-Sturmbrigade neuer Art*, which was organized as follows:

Brigade headquarters
I. Bataillon
1st – 3rd Rifle Companies
4th (heavy) Company
5th (anti-tank) Company
Brigade Units
(Infantry Gun) Company
(Assault Gun) Battery
(20 mm Flak) Battery
(88 mm Flak) Battery

SS-Hauptsturmführer Erich Kostenbader, former commander of *2./SS-Regiment (mot.) "Deutschland,"* was initially named commanding officer. After, on the one hand, the heavy support units could not be formed or consisted only of personnel due to a lack of equipment, and, on the other, just under 700 volunteers had received pre-training in Sennheim, a so-called training battalion was formed at the SS training camp in Bohemia. Commander of this battalion was the former French Lt. Col. Gamory-Duboureau. Born in 1885, he had taken part in the 1st Special Course in Tölz as an *SS-Hauptsturmführer*. After completing the course he had been promoted to *SS-Sturmbannführer*.

Together with French-speaking Wallonian volunteers, the members of the training battalion took part in the "First French Waffen-Junker Course" at the SS Panzer Grenadier School in Kienschlag from May 7 to September 9, 1944. A preparatory course was also held for French and Wallonian volunteers from August 24–30 to November 1944, and it was followed by the "Second French Waffen-Junker Course" from December 1, 1944, to

Waffen-Grenadier Henri Simon.

Waffen-Obersturmführer Dr. Rene Fraysee.

Volunteers were accepted up to the age of forty years.

February 5, 1945. Another preparatory course began on February 5, and ended on April 14, 1945. Because the end of the war was so close, the planned "Third French Waffen-Junker Course" (April 15 to August 15, 1945) was not held.

In addition to the just under 1,700 Frenchmen in the Protectorate of Bohemia and Moravia, there was also the *(französische) I. Bataillon* (French I Battalion) at the SS training camp in Sennheim. It had a strength of about 1,000 recruits, volunteers taken in in the spring of 1944. The battalion commander, *SS-Sturmbannführer* Hersche from Switzerland, tried to bring order to what he described as a "corrupt and undisciplined gang." In the process, even some of the German instructors were replaced. Typically, they had behaved badly in their tone and manner of behavior towards the French volunteers. As a result, entire groups left without leave. As well, underage volunteers who had been "conned" by the recruiting committees were discharged.[11] During an inspection of the camp on July 21, 1944, *SS-Obergruppenführer* Berger, head of the *SS-Hauptamt*, spoke the following empty phrases to Hersche:[12]

> What I have seen today proves to me that there are only three nations in Europe that are soldiers, the Germans, the Swiss and the French. The battalion I have inspected today is made up of Frenchmen, it is trained and led by a Swiss officer and according to the principles of the German Army. The battalion stands comparison with any German unit.[13]

On July 30, 1944, the unit—less the French battalion in Sennheim—had:

Officers	NCOs	Enlisted Men	Total
30	44	1,614	1,688
1.78%	2.61%	95.61%	100%

Particularly striking is the relationship between the noncommissioned officers and enlisted men. The numbers reveal that the planned recruitment or training of almost 400 French officers and noncommissioned officers could not be accomplished.

Notwithstanding this, another fifty-five French officers and noncommissioned officers—most from the militia, were recruited for training or retraining according to German regulations at the newly established SS Grenadier School in Sophienwalde (West Prussia).

The first action followed the launching of the Soviet summer offensive on June 22, 1944. A one-week maneuver was subsequently held at the SS training camp in Bohemia in the second week of July. This was also the *I. Bataillon*'s final inspection. It was expected that, after about a year of training, the battalion would be operational. When the Soviets launched a major attack towards Lvov on July 16, 1944, the French volunteers were confined to barracks, and after the Red Army took Lvov, Yaroslavl and Przemsyl on July 28, the *SS-Führungshauptamt* ordered the formation of an approximately 1,000-man-strong battle group. It was to be sent to the *18. SS-Freiwilligen-Panzergrenadier-Division "Horst Wessel,"* which had suffered heavily in the previous fighting, in the Przemsyl area.

Apart from a few anti-tank guns, the SS battle group had received no heavy weapons. It therefore consisted almost entirely of infantrymen of the *I./Französische SS-Freiwilligen-Sturmbrigade* under the command of *SS-Hauptsturmführer* Cance (aide-de-camp: *SS-Untersturmführer* Scapula). The German liaison staff was commanded by *SS-Obersturmführer* Reiche. The companies were commanded by:

Headquarters Company	*SS-Obersturmführer* Criosille
1st Company	*SS-Obersturmführer* de Tissot
2nd Company	*SS-Untersturmführer* Gauthier
3rd Company	*SS-Obersturmführer* Fenet
4th Company	*SS-Obersturmführer* Ferney[14]
5th (Anti-Tank) Company	*SS-Obersturmführer* Pleyber

Prior to leaving for the eastern front, a French SS volunteer wrote a farewell letter to his parents. It reveals how split many French families were about their sons volunteering to serve in the Waffen-SS:[15]

> My dear parents,
>
> I presume that you have received my letter in which I informed you that I have signed up with the Waffen-SS for the duration of the war. I always had this idea, and I also know that you hold a different view. But, dear parents, one should never act against his ideals.
>
> Perhaps your home is forever closed to me, but if anything ever happens to you I will be the first to rush to your aid, if it is not already too late. Remember that, despite everything, I will love you always. A

child must always love his parents; they have enough difficulty getting us far enough that we can later earn our own keep.

I will soon be going to the front and I believe that as Frenchmen who have worked continuously and hard, you will someday be able to be proud to have given your son for his ideal—the defense of France and all of Europe.

My dear old parents, I do not believe that in the end you will have anything to reproach me for.

André Bayle described the move to the eastern front:

On July 15, 1944, we were confined to barracks in Neweklau, having completed a weeklong maneuver under the inspection of senior officers. They confirmed that the battalion was battle-ready and praised our enthusiasm and good level of training. We then had to prepare our combat equipment, leaving out all personal things or anything not included in the service regulations. The surplus items, marked with out names, were packaged and left with the baggage train. The ultimate composition of individual units had also not yet been decided. Thought also had to be given to the command forces of the *II. Bataillon*, which was supposed to reinforce us …

And then came the big day. The trucks that were supposed to take us to the station were late arriving, but the best that Cance could come up with was to march us to Beneschau, where we were to board the train. We, the "motorized ones," marched off, which for us, given our training and future actions at the front, was no change. March endlessly and without rest was to become our motto …

There was no band for our departure. There were obviously mixed feelings of joy and uncertainty in our heads, everyone's thoughts strayed far from this Bohemian land, which we were sorry to leave.

The stations passed by—Tabor, Iglau, Brünn, the capital city of the Protectorate of Moravia, then Bratislava, the capital of Slovakia, which had become a free and sovereign state and whose soldiers gave us a friendly greeting.

We were now in the West Carpathians, in Slovakia, where we were forbidden to leave the area of the railroad tracks: the German military had only been granted the right of transit. At every stop the population gave us flowers and white bread, something we hadn't seen since the start of the war …

Then our journey continued through Nova Zamky, Nagykalna, Lucenec, Miscolc in Hungary, then through Hidaspemen and Muncacs into the Ukraine. From the latter we then steamed west again, to Oshgorod, then northeast to Turka, our destination.

After a difficult six-day ride through the Carpathians—with two locomotives and on grades, which often led to uncoupling of the cars and, once in a tunnel, to the division of our train into three—we arrived in Turka.

Waffen-Standarten-Oberjunker Abel Chaby.

French SS volunteers at the Bohemia troop training camp.

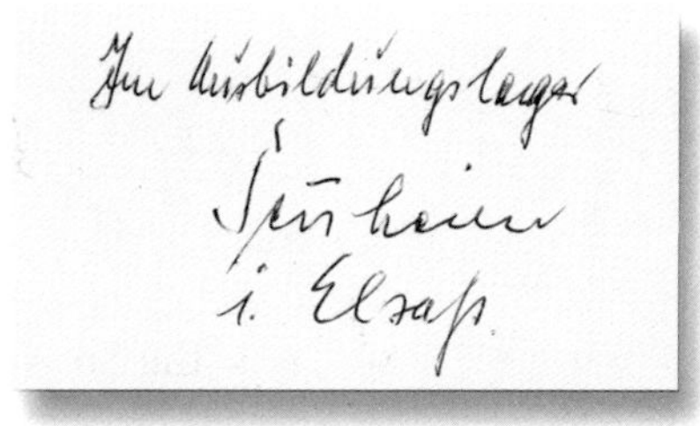

SS-Obergruppenführer Berger, head of the *SS-Hauptamt*, during a visit to the SS training camp in Sennheim. Concerning the French SS volunteers, he wrote to *SS-Gruppenführer* Oberg, the Senior SS and Police Commander in France: "No German mother will weep for any foreigner who falls."

One hundred and fifty SS volunteers were killed in Galicia (below), fifty were listed missing and 660 were wounded. It is believed that 400 French troops were killed in Pomerania and about 4,000 were wounded or taken prisoner by the Soviets.

Action in Galicia

Within a few weeks, the Soviet summer offensive that began on June 22, 1944, resulted in the total collapse of the fronts held by the German Army Groups Center and North Ukraine. Such was the personnel and materiel superiority of the Red Army that the *Wehrmacht* could do little against it. While the German newspapers initially reported that:

> The Bolsheviks have begun their expected attack in the central sector. The attacks, made on a broad front with tank and air support, were repulsed in heavy fighting and local penetrations were immediately cleaned up by immediate counterattacks. Fierce fighting is still in progress on both sides of Vitebsk.

The report on July 28, 1944, showed that the Soviets had gained an enormous amount of ground in barely five weeks:

> On the Eastern Front, the big defensive battle between the Carpathians and the Gulf of Finland has grown in ferocity. After the enemy succeeded in driving deep into our front in various sectors, salients in several sectors were abandoned to preserve forces. In the course of these adjustments of the front, the cities of Lvov, Brest-Litovsk, Bialystok and Dvinsk were abandoned after all militarily important installations were destroyed.

On July 28, 1944, the French SS Volunteer Assault Brigade was placed on alert. One week later the battalion arrived at Stryj in the *Generalgouvernement* and the next day set out on foot for Sanok, eighty kilometers to the northwest. There the units were supposed to be attached to the *18. SS-Freiwilligen-Panzer-Grenadier-Division "Horst Wessel,"* which was heavily engaged. To hasten the arrival of these reinforcements, on August 7, the division dispatched trucks to collect the French troops approaching on foot. In this way the volunteers reached the *XXIV. Panzer-Korps* in the Sanok area (approximately fifty kilometers southwest of Przemsyl) in the afternoon. The next evening division commander *SS-Oberführer* Trabandt briefed *SS-Hauptsturmführer* Cance on the situation and attached the battalion to SS Battle Group Schäfer.

Operating within *Armee-Gruppe Generaloberst Heinrici* (*1. Panzer-Armee* and 1st Hungarian Army), its orders were to restore contact with the *17. Armee* situated to the north, which had been broken by the Soviet advance.

On August 9–10, the French volunteers occupied the area south of Pisarowce (approximately eight kilometers west of Sanok) and tried to establish contact with the *208. Infanterie-Division* on their left. Under heavy enemy artillery and mortar fire, the units suffered heavy casualties while moving into their jump-off position in the area of the forest around Dudynce. The assault towards Pisarowce began on August 12, 1944, after heavy preparatory fire, the objective being to restore the road link from Cracow to Sanok. The villages of Pielna and Dudynce were occupied. The assault on Pisarowce followed three days later. André Bayle remembered that August 15, 1944:

> Today is Tuesday, the 15th of August, it is very early in the morning. Just now the Allies are landing on the coast of my beloved Provence.
>
> While Pleyber and Peyron try to obtain definite information about the enemy situation, we sit down by the side of the road to eat breakfast. We have unpacked our field equipment and the men have divided themselves into small groups of friends. Believing we are still far from the front, we post no sentries and are still sitting in the ditches on both sides of the road leading to the village (Pisarowce).
>
> Suddenly we hear firing from the east, but we are not concerned. We curse the early "hunters" who might possibly hit us, and those of us who are eating breakfast in the ditch on the west side cross the road to take cover in the other ditch just to be safe. At that instant the acting company commander and the platoon leader, who is from Marseille, come running from the direction of the village. They shouted something to us that we did not immediately understand: "The Reds! The Reds!" They point towards the wheat fields east of the road, from where the enemy intends to make a surprise attack.
>
> Well prepared thanks to our excellent training, we immediately collect our gear and form our squads for the attack. Without waiting for orders, everyone has fixed bayonets and now stares at the wheat fields. Next to me a young grenadier takes a bullet in the armpit just as he straightens up to look for the enemy. Blood spurts from his shoulder and he collapses without saying a word.

André Bayle.

Members of *I./Französische SS-Freiwilligen-Sturmbrigade* in the summer of 1944.

When Peyron is again in our midst, he orders "forwards!" and is the first to run through the wheat. We see nothing, but now we can hear our artillery. Rifle bullets are whizzing over and past us and we run as if on exercise, throwing ourselves down every twenty meters. We emerge from the wheat field and see the enemy beginning to flee.

Needing a cigarette to calm his nerves, my comrade Raymond, who instead of his MP40 is still armed only with a bayonet, asks me for a light even though he knows that I am a non-smoker. That's probably because of the tremendous excitement! As I lie there I see the very young Saccoman hit in mid stride and fall.

There are many wounded, who are now being looked after, and dead on both sides. We must continue on. We move into what is left of the village and fire one- and two-star flares, the signal to shift fire forward, otherwise our unit's rapid advance will result in casualties from our own guns.

We wrest the first houses from the enemy and search them. We find Soviet officers' uniforms, equipment, even hot food. At the entrances to the cellars and houses we call: "Ida souda," which means "come out." Incidentally I have never known if that was right. In any case we toss hand grenades into the cellar rooms. We mow down everything and the enemy flees.

We come to a small slow-moving stream. There are tall trees and it is warm. A beautiful summer day! It is the feast of Mary most Holy, the Assumption of Mary.

We watch several Russians moving a mobile machine-gun into position in a wood. Peyron instructs us to attack the enemy before they can open fire. At the same moment I hear Trévisan, who is also from Marseille, calling for help behind us. I rush to him and find that he has been hit in the back, in the area of the kidneys. He is bleeding and I have red hands. Peyron turns round and orders me to stop. "It's no use," he says. Trévisan dies as I join Peyron to help destroy the Russian machine-gun, which is about thirty meters away. Peyron leads the assault and is the first to start running. Then I see our platoon leader killed by a mortar fragment.

I want to collect Peyron's papers and his MP40, but I immediately come under fire. I have no more ammunition and would liked to have taken Peyron's clip. Instead I pick up a Russian PPSH 41 submachine-gun. Ammunition for it was easy to find. With my squad I resumed the advance and finally reach the rail crossing, where we stop. I see Raymond

> at the head of the platoon, and from a distance we agree to halt the French advance at the rail line and wait for further orders. As we no longer have an officer and have no idea what our mission is from here, we must wait for orders or go get them. But how?
>
> While we are deliberating what to do, a German officer, an army tank major, approaches our position at the rail crossing and asks who is in command there.
>
> I introduce myself and explain our situation, whereupon the major declares that we have reached the objective, of which we had been unaware. As I was the only one who spoke enough German, in the rubble of the village called Pisarowce I go to a signals unit and try to make radio contact with my battalion.

The very next day the battalion was relieved within the *18. SS-Freiwilligen-Panzer-Grenadier-Division "Horst Wessel"* by the *68. Infanterie-Division* and assembled in the Dukla–Novy Zmigrod area (about forty kilometers west of Pisarowce). From there, on August 17, it was moved by truck approximately eighty kilometers north into the Mielec area on the Visloka River, in the sector of the *LIX. Armee-Korps* (*17. Armee*). The battalion had suffered casualties of about 130 killed and wounded in the fighting in the Pisarowce area, which was equivalent to the loss of almost an entire company.

In the new area of operations along the Visloka, the *17. Armee* was already awaiting a major attack in the direction of Cracow by the Red Army. Under the command of the *18. SS-Freiwilligen-Panzer-Grenadier-Division "Horst Wessel,"* the French SS volunteers were supposed to take over a previously quiet sector from the Wehrmacht. The battalion headquarters took up position in Zaborcze (approximately five kilometers northwest of Przeclaw), while the companies took over positions on the left bank of the Visloka between Mielec and Przeclaw.

After three relatively quiet days, on August 20, 1944, the enemy launched his expected offensive after a two-hour artillery barrage. With Soviet tanks advancing towards Radomysl Wielky south of the French positions, the last remaining anti-tank guns under the command of *SS-Oberjunker* Kreis were ordered there. Forming an improvised battle group, they held the town until reinforcements arrived.

After back and forth fighting on the line Radomysl Wielky–Przeclaw, the grenadier companies were forced to withdraw. During the fighting, the 1st Company was encircled in Przeclaw. A relief attempt by *SS-Panzer-*

Aufklärungs-Abteilung 18 (SS Armored Reconnaissance Battalion 18) was unsuccessful. Company commander *SS-Obersturmführer* de Tissot was killed in the fighting. Under extremely heavy fire, during the night of August 22, 1944, the French volunteers assembled near Mokre (approximately five kilometers southwest of Przeclaw). The Red Army immediately followed up and there was heavy close-quarters fighting near this village, in which *SS-Obersturmführer* Pleyber, commander of the 2nd Company, was killed. With the soldiers already running out of ammunition, they were left with little more than spades, bayonets and rifle butts with which to defend themselves in the hand-to-hand fighting.

The French abandoned Mokre during the night of August 23, and withdrew towards Debica, roughly ten kilometers away.[16] There they fought off several attacks by the enemy and on August 24, severely mauled, were pulled out of the front. The remnants of the battalion were initially trucked to Pilzno, about ten kilometers away. From there they continued to the rest area in Tarnow. The battalion had suffered huge losses in just under a week. Counting the losses before Pisarowce, a total of 130 volunteers had been killed, about fifty were missing and 660 had been wounded.

These numbers are a reflection of the fact that the Red Army had attacked with a materiel superiority in artillery, mortars, tanks and aircraft, against which the Wehrmacht could do nothing. The infantrymen were immediately forced out of their positions and for almost four days were driven across the open plains. The repeated halt orders resulted in numerous close-quarters battles with further heavy casualties. All of this ultimately led to the French soldiers, like their German counterparts, fighting for their very survival.

After achieving its objectives, the Red Army halted its attacks. On the same day (September 1, 1944)—the fifth anniversary of the start of the war—as the remnants of the battalion were moving by rail to Greifenberg, the Wehrmacht communiqué reported euphemistically:

> On the Eastern Front the Bolshevik summer offensive has been halted before a continuous front between the eastern Carpathians and the Gulf of Finland.

In fact the enemy had gained more than 400 kilometers of ground toward the west and had established bridgeheads across the Vistula and the Narev. It had thus created jumping-off positions for its spring 1945 offensive.

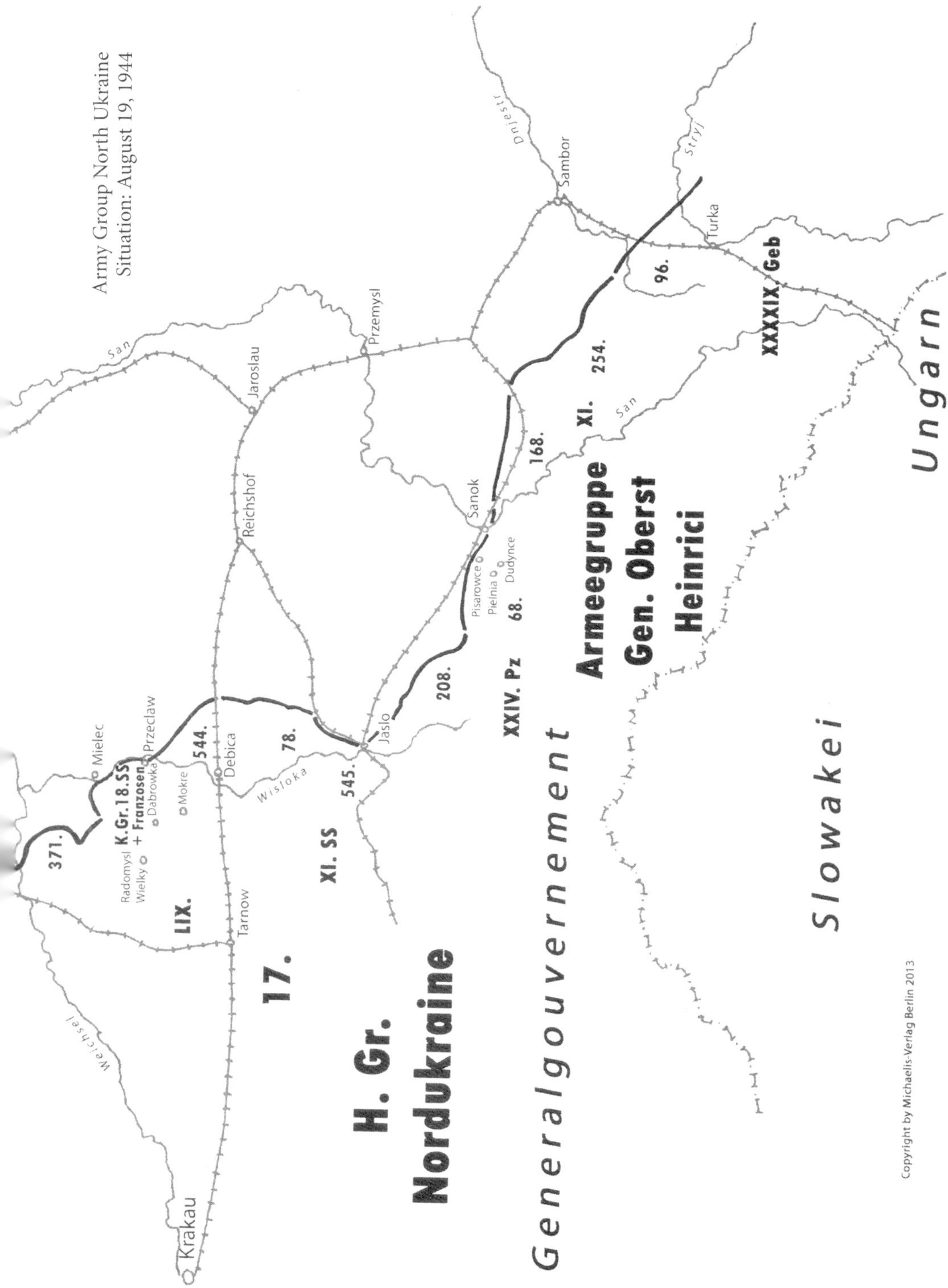
Army Group North Ukraine
Situation: August 19, 1944
H. Gr.
Nordukraine
17.
LIX.
XI. SS
371.
K.Gr.18.SS
+ Franzosen
544.
78.
545.
208.
XXIV. Pz
68.
168.
XI.
254.
96.
XXXXIX. Geb
Armeegruppe
Gen. Oberst
Heinrici
Generalgouvernement
Slowakei
Ungarn
Krakau
Tarnow
Radomysl
Wielky
Mielec
Przeclaw
Dabrowka
Mokre
Debica
Wisloka
Weichsel
Jaslo
Reichshof
Jaroslau
Przemysl
San
Sanok
Pisarowce
Pielnia
Dudynce
Sambor
Dnjestr
Stryj
Turka

While the German units prepared as best they could for the next major offensive by the Soviets by building positions and training, the Red Army began building up its forces opposite Army Groups Center and A (designated Army Group North Ukraine until September 23, 1944) to the level that made breaking through the German lines a certainty.

André Bayle recalled the fighting and the heavy casualties during operations in the *Generalgouvernement*:

> We had to follow the others (those retreating), but the Ivans appeared everywhere. Nevertheless we made it, and at about noon, on reaching the new resistance line, we joined Barto and our 2nd Company, which we had found again. This enabled the 3rd Company, after losing its 3rd Platoon, to fight its way through to us. Losses on both sides were very high. Some of our comrades were also taken prisoner.
>
> The retreat was difficult … We split up to make the retreat easier. Agreed rendezvous point was the village of Mokre, where Cance was supposed to have set up his command post … Large numbers of Russians had already infiltrated into the position envisaged for our units. Night came, and as we began digging holes for the night, trucks approached with their headlights on. The Soviet soldiers were talking loudly, exercising no caution. They were really self-confident and conscious of their strength.
>
> We moved out before dawn, to escape the attention of our nocturnal neighbors. The dense fog concealed us, but it also made orientation difficult. Luckily we came upon one of the few signs that showed a direction: "Mokre three kilometers." We stumbled onto one of our forward outposts and they showed us a road that led straight to Cance's command post.
>
> The fog gradually lifted in the early forenoon, and we were ordered to reinforce our comrades. The first I met was Reiche. Our young German liaison officer briefed me on the situation while kneeling and peering through his binoculars. It really wasn't rosy.
>
> A runner brought the order for us to retreat, which was to be carried out en masse without attracting the enemy's attention. Then I learned of the death of one of the sons of General Staff Officer Croisille, who had been with us in Posen (the other son was killed in Berlin), the death of *SS-Untersturmführer* Lamert, whose chest had been pierced twice, of *Oberscharführer* Pouget, with a shell fragment in his chest, of Mamet, an outstanding machine-gunner, of Laroche, the radio operator, of *Untersturmführer* Scapula and his driver, killed when a *panzerfaust*

exploded in their vehicle, and the wounding of many comrades. It was nearly a catastrophe for our unit. The orders were given and everyone began creeping backwards, which impeded the retreat, even though we had practiced it sufficiently …

Suddenly I saw that Cance had been wounded. He limped over to his *Kübelwagen*, holding his knee. Raymond, who was carrying a wounded man on his back, was knocked to the ground by a nearby explosion. Wounded, he tried to stand up, and was picked up by Cance's vehicle. The wounded man Raymond had been carrying was killed by a shell fragment.

We neared the battalion command post and watched as Reiche, Le Marquer and Binder (the second liaison officer) went into the farmhouse. At that instant a salvo struck the farmhouse and all were killed.

Enemy tanks carrying infantry came closer and closer. Suddenly an army officer came running with a beautiful German shepherd dog. He had lost his belt, his helmet and his weapon and was screaming "Ivan's coming, Ivan's coming!," but he was pointing in a different direction than that from which the Russians were attacking with their tanks. Panic immediately broke out among the wounded on the farm. They tried to run away, but in vain. They fell, their bandages loosened and, covered in blood, they died. The tank attack took place at the same moment. They opened up with everything they had and spread panic among those who had previously got away, and many were killed. Almost all of the dead were on that farm, and, staggering, I ran away.

We met army soldiers who were making a counterattack. Smiling, they greeted us with handshakes. Those left of us assembled at the battalion baggage train with its officers Croiselle, Maud'huit, Neubauer, *SS-Oberscharführer* Pruvost and the doctor Bonnefoye.

Our retreat was now made by truck to Tarnow, where we were able to rest for a week and indulge ourselves. The entire battalion's field rations for the last two weeks was now available to we 140 escapees!

Despite the immediate aftereffect and proximity of the fighting, the din of which still rang in our ears, we tried to relax. On September 1, 1944, we climbed onto the train in Tarnow, east of Cracow, that was to take us to Schwarnegast for the formation of the Charlemagne Brigade. It took four days to make that roughly 600-kilometer journey, and on September 5, we arrived at Bruss Station. It was seventeen kilometers from Camp Schwarnegast, and the *II. Bataillon* from Neweklau and the French training battalion from Sennheim were already there.

The *Waffen-Grenadier-Brigade der SS "Charlemagne" (Französische Nr. 1)*

While the first French SS volunteers were in combat on the eastern front, on August 10, 1944, orders were issued for the merging of the French Volunteer Legion (*Légion des volontaires français contre le bolchévisme – LVF*), which was under army command, and the French SS Volunteer Assault Brigade into the "*Französischen Brigade der SS*" (French SS Brigade).[17]

Prior to this, discussions had taken place between the former commander of the French *Grenadier-Regiment 638*, *Oberst* Puaud, and Himmler in Berlin. The *Reichsführer-SS* explained that Hitler had instructed him to combine all of the foreigners serving in the Waffen-SS for reasons of simplification and better organization. After the assassination attempt on Hitler on July 20, 1944, Himmler had been named Commander of the Replacement Army, and this now stood him in good stead. As *Oberst* Puaud was presented with a fait accompli, there was nothing left for him to do but pledge the loyalty of the members of *Grenadier-Regiment 638*. Beyond that, it was surely clear to him that this combination of forces made sense. As he was named *Waffen-Oberführer* and commander of the brigade by Himmler—effective September 1, 1944—his French volunteers, formerly under the army, did not just simply "drop" into the Waffen-SS.

In addition, from mid-September 1944, approximately 1,200 French Kriegsmarine volunteers, who hitherto had been combined into *Schiffs-Stamm-Abteilung 28* at the SS training camp in Sennheim, arrived at the "Westpreußen" training camp, which had been selected for formation of the brigade. With little motivation to serve in the Waffen-SS and potentially fight on the eastern front, *Waffen-Oberführer* Puaud incorporated these former members of the Kriegsmarine more into the supply and staff units than the fighting forces.

In October 1944 the French SS Brigade was renamed ***Waffen-Grenadier-Brigade der Waffen-SS "Charlemagne."*** It was now designated a "***Waffen-Verband der SS***" which indicated a new rating by the *SS-Führungshauptamt*. With the incorporation of numerous men "not fit for the SS," most of the Frenchmen were not representative of "more German-related volunteers." The rank designations for the former SS volunteers also changed, from *SS-Unterscharführer* to *Waffen-Unterscharführer* for example. In February 1944,

*SS-Obergruppenf*ührer Berger, head of the *SS-Hauptamt*, described his opinion of taking in such men in a letter to *SS-Gruppenführer* Oberg, senior SS and police commander France. His statements were banal:[18]

> I myself—I would like to say this to you quite personally—take the position that it is a crime if we do not at the present time make use of all the forces ready to fight for us. No German mother will cry for any foreigner who is killed! I tell you this on the day of my son's death.

After Germany was unable in early 1944 to equip the French SS Volunteer Assault Brigade with all the needed heavy weapons (for example an assault gun battery), the unit was immediately organized as a grenadier brigade. Because of their length of time they had been engaged in training and formation, the French volunteers were certainly not "cannon fodder," however heavy supporting weapons and equipment were assigned mainly to the SS panzer divisions. Without this equipment, however, successful action at the front, as the fighting behind the Visloka had shown, was practically impossible. The brigade was to be organized as follows:

Combat Units

Brigade Headquarters

Waffen-Grenadier-Regiment der SS[19] *(französische Nr. 1)*

I. Bataillon with 1st – 3rd Rifle Companies and 4th (Heavy) Company

II. Bataillon with 5th – 7th Rifle Companies and 8th (Heavy Company)

Waffen-Grenadier-Regiment der SS (französische Nr. 2) as the first regiment

SS-Panzerjäger-Abteilung 57 with

1 heavy anti-tank gun company (75 mm motorized)

1 assault gun company

1 flak Company (37 mm)

SS-Artillerie-Abteilung 57 with 3 batteries of 105 mm light field howitzers

Mixed *SS-Nachrichten-Kompanie 57* (signals)

SS-Pionier-Kompanie 57

SS-Feldersatz-Bataillon 57 (replacement battalion)

Supply Units

2 60-ton motor transport troops
SS-Feldpostamt 57 (field post office)
SS-Werkstatt-Kp. 57 with 1 workshop and 1 armorer platoon
SS-Sanitäts-Kompanie 57 (medical company)
SS-Veterinär-Kompanie 57 (veterinary company)

The first regiment (commander: *Waffen-Obersturmbannführer* Gamory-Dubourdeau) was formed from the remnants of the French SS Volunteer Assault Brigade that returned from action and from the training battalion. The second regiment (commander: *Waffen-Hauptsturmführer* Bridoux) was formed from French Grenadier Regiment 638 transferred from the army, during which the *II. Bataillon* was disbanded and its personnel divided among the former *I.* and *III. Bataillon*. The two supporting companies of the SS Volunteer Assault Brigade joined the *Panzerjäger-Abteilung* (commander: *Waffen-Hauptsturmführer* de Vaugelas), while the 2nd (Assault Gun) Company consisted of personnel only with no assault guns.

There was also a German command staff with three officers—one of them with the disciplinary authority of a brigade commander—two noncommissioned officers and four enlisted men. The French-speaking *SS-Oberführer* Dr. Krukenberg was named to command this German liaison staff. He was to be the primary advisor to the French brigade commander in all matters of training and command of the brigade as well as the disciplinary superior of the brigade's German personnel. Essentially these were the German liaison staffs to the individual units. Two German officers, two NCOs and two enlisted men were to be attached to each regimental headquarters and one of each to the headquarters of battalions and independent battalions. Most administrative positions—such as the accounting officer, for example—were to be filled by German personnel.

On October 10, 1944, the Inspectorate of French SS Units was created from the operations staff. Krukenberg was promoted to *SS-Brigadeführer* and named inspector. One of his important tasks was to smooth out the existing discrepancies between the members of the various French organizations together with *Waffen-Oberführer* Puaud.

In some cases the men refused to accept transfer to the Waffen-SS, and in some cases there were tensions among the French personnel—like those that already existed between the right-wing organizations in France. After

SS-Brigadeführer Dr. Krukenberg—Inspector of French SS Units. He is seen here while still a member of the Wehrmacht.

SS-Standartenführer Zimmermann, commander of *Waffen-Grenadier-Regiment der SS "Charlemagne,"* Christmas 1944.

the language of command and orders in the French SS Volunteer Assault Brigade had been German, the members of the LVF accused the SS volunteers, for example, of having betrayed French military tradition. And in fact it was rather paradoxical when two Frenchmen faced each other and gave or received a report in broken German. Even worse was the singing of German marching songs, during which the soldiers did not even understand the meaning of the words. André Bayle described this:

> In Neweklau and elsewhere, however, singing was the nightmare of most French volunteers within the Waffen-SS. Several former pathfinders like me had previously sung in groups; there were even tenors from Corsica or Toulouse there. Nevertheless the Frenchmen hummed the foreign words of the German songs to themselves without any emphasis. For many it became torture.

And with respect to the problem regarding the LVF he remembered:

> In Schwarnegast, Barno took over command of the last 140 members of the battalion, even though he had an injured leg. He decided that the approximately 100 less seriously wounded would be transported away, using the trucks that were supposed to fetch our equipment from the train. He himself rode in a Volkswagen. Barto summoned me and placed me in command of the "remnant" battalion. I took command of a unit of just forty emaciated men.
>
> After the trucks and Barto had driven off, we set out on the seventeen-kilometer march. After about five or six kilometers, which meant we were near the base of our comrades of the LVF, I saw a rider trotting along. From his shoulder tabs and the tricolored France emblem above his right elbow, I soon recognized the rider as a captain of the LVF. When the captain neared our group, I had the men correct their posture and pace and finally presented to him my "battalion," which continued marching in a very disciplined manner. When I reached him I gave my name, my rank, my temporary function and the unit, all in German in accordance with Waffen-SS regulations.
>
> The bewildered Gaul reacted in the typical manner of the French army, which meant that he shouted at me (in French), asking if it was my intention to muck around with him. I replied in French that I was following the Waffen-SS regulations. He demanded that I present my

unit in French whether I liked it or not. I had no choice but to follow the order to respect discipline and hierarchy and said: "*SS-Unterscharführer* Bayle, commander of the 1st Battalion of the Assault Brigade of French Volunteers of the Waffen-SS with forty men."

No sooner had the captain heard this, when he began to yell that I was pulling his leg and that I hadn't heard the last of it! Then he turned around and galloped away, without saluting.

As part of the attempt to form a relatively homogenous unit, at the beginning of October 1944, brigade commander *Waffen-Oberführer* Puaud was instructed to perform security checks on his men, especially the members of the Kriegsmarine, who were not in action. As a result, on October 11, more than eighty Frenchmen were placed on a "list of undesirables." Depending on their transgression and appearance, they were either sent to the SS and Police Penal Camp in Danzig–Matzkau or to a labor camp. The most common reasons for this were:

- unauthorized absence from their unit or desertion
- theft
- making defeatist statements
- listening to forbidden radio stations
- bad attitude
- questionable character
- lack of discipline
- communist propaganda

The move from West Prussia to the Wildflecken training camp in the Rhön Mountains began at the end of the month. While the former training battalion, now the *II. Bataillon* of the French SS Volunteer Assault Brigade had spent just about two months at the West Prussia training camp, the *I. (französische) Bataillon* of the SS Training Camp and now *Französische Grenadier-Ausbildungs- und Ersatz-Bataillon der SS* (French SS Grenadier Training and Replacement Battalion) remained in Greifenberg until February 14, 1945, and only then was transferred to Wildflecken to escape the advancing Red Army.[20]

On November 5, 1944, approximately 1,500 members of the militia also arrived there. In late September, early October 1944, there had been several discussions between Darnand, leader of the militia, and *SS-Obergruppenführer* Berger, head of the *SS-Hauptamt*, about incorporating the militia members

Training and swearing in of French SS volunteers at Wildflecken.

into the brigade at the Heuberg training camp. The men thus again found employment after leaving France. This also made it possible to fill several command positions within the brigade. For example, the former militia officers and now *Waffen-Hauptsturmführer* de Bourmont and Basompierre were sent on battalion commander courses. The remaining militia members took the oath to Adolf Hitler on November 12, 1944 in the presence of their leader Darnand.[21]

If the combination of the LVF and the French Kriegsmarine volunteers with the French SS Volunteer Assault Brigade had resulted in problems, they grew even worse with the addition of the militia members. The eastern front volunteers often looked down on the militiamen as the latter had seen themselves as warriors against communism in the homeland, while they had lived through the cold, heat and powder smoke in the USSR. On the other hand, the militiamen accused the soldiers of having become German mercenaries instead of fighting communism at home in French uniforms. When the, in some cases barely relevant, ranks of the militiamen were simply converted into the military ranks of the Waffen-SS, this also drew protests from those who had experienced the tough courses at the SS weapons and officer schools. As the men lacked basic German-style military training, they were distributed among the brigade in small groups. Clothing the militiamen also caused problems. The majority were issued worn-out clothing, captured uniforms or even misappropriate items of equipment from the SA or *Postschutz*.

In November 1944, about 1,700 French members of the *Organisation Todt* (OT), most in the associated so-called *Schutzkommandos* (guard detachments) also arrived at the training camp. They had guarded the OT workers and construction sites in France and had been evacuated with the Germans when they left France. The bulk of these men were unfit for any kind of military employment.

After the arrival of the members of the Kriegsmarine, the *Organisation Todt* and the militia, the brigade's composition was as follows. It consisted of about 7,500 men:

1,900 were members of the French SS Volunteer Assault Brigade and
1,200 were members of the French Grenadier Regiment 638 (LVF)
1,200 were members of the Kriegsmarine
1,500 were members of the French Militia
1,700 were members of the *Organisation Todt Schutzkommandos*

After a conversation with *SS-Sturmbannführer* Degrelle, *SS-Gruppenführer* von Pückler, Waffen-SS Commander Bohemia-Moravia wrote the following in a letter to *SS-Obergruppenführer* Frank, German minister of state for Bohemia and Moravia, concerning the political origins of the men:

> (*SS-Obersturmbannführer*) Gamory-Dubourdeau is a member of the executive of the Parti populaire and is trying to prove that the majority of the French volunteers belong to his party and not to the militia assembled by Darnand. Degrelle disagrees and estimates 30% Parti populaire, 30% militia and 40% with no political opinion. (Seems likely.)

As about 600 members of the militia joined the French SS Volunteer Regiment in 1943 and the organization later provided more volunteers, one can in fact assume that, with the approximately 1,500 militiamen from Heuberg, the militia made up about 30% of the brigade. The bulk of the volunteers from the Kriegsmarine, the OT guard detachments and elements of the LVF could be seen as politically non-active and made up about 40% of the brigade, therefore about 30% must have been members of the *Parti populaire*. The estimate by *Wallonian Rexist* leader Leon Degrelle was thus quite accurate.

Already on November 21, 1944, *SS-Gruppenführer* von Pückler reported on the very interesting statements by *SS-Sturmbannführer* Degrelle about basic errors in German policy in the occupied territories in the east and west (especially Belgium and France):

> *SS-Sturmbannführer* Degrelle was here in the Protectorate for two days to visit the Wallonian volunteers in the schools. His visit to his own men left behind a very strong impression. This was also true of the Frenchmen, several of whom were present. In my opinion Degrelle, a trained speaker, could also be used very effectively on the French and Flemish. He has what it takes, and his high decorations and rapid rise in the Waffen-SS make him particularly suitable.
>
> I have twice had Degrelle as a guest. He spoke to me very openly and touched on several points that I think important:

1.) Basic mistakes in our political and economic administration in the occupied western territories. Degrelle was very sharp in his criticism. In particular he criticized several senior army officers, especially Falkenhausen …
Mistakes have also been made by the Waffen-SS. For example, he said: "How can we entrust the history of our land to an officer who cannot speak a word of our language, who does not know our literature, our spiritual life and our mentality, and who has never been in our land." (He was obviously referring to SS-Obergruppenführer Berger.)
2.) (…)
3.) From his own experience in the east he gave a number of unpleasant examples, especially concerning the German civil administration.
4.) An account of a visit to Sigmaringen with Marshal Petain and various members of the so-called French government, all of whom were squabbling amongst themselves, but who were also repeatedly played off or supported one against the other by various German officials, was very amusing. The Reich Foreign Minister, *SS-Obergruppenführer* Berger and the German ambassador were all pulling different strings. The details of his visit were extremely humorous.

Degrelle was obviously seen as a possible political figurehead who could unite and represent the French-Belgian collaboration militarily and politically.

Much to everyone's surprise, at the beginning of December 1944 *Waffen-Sturmbannführer* Bridoux, commander of *Waffen-Grenadier-Regiment der SS 58 (französische Nr. 2)*, formerly of the LVF, left the brigade. His father, Lt. Gen. Bridoux (under-secretary of state in the government of Marshal Pétain), had recently visited him and probably spurred him to leave the sinking ship while there was still time. Bridoux gave the same advice to his officers and encouraged them to follow his example.

When *Waffen-Obersturmbannführer* Gamory-Dubourdeau, leader of *Waffen-Grenadier-Regiment der SS 57 (franz. Nr. 1)*, also relinquished his position and moved to the *SS-Hauptamt*, two *Waffen-Hauptsturmführer* took over command of the regiments. They were Victor de Boumont, born in 1907 and formerly the chief of militia in Lyon, and Emile Raybaud, born in 1910 in Tans and a former officer in the Alpine Corps.

In addition to the basic infantry training given the new recruits, who were severely limited by winter weather conditions as well as inadequate clothing and food, many soldiers—most former members or the Kriegsmarine or the *Organisation Todt*—were sent to the various Waffen-SS training and replacement units and schools.

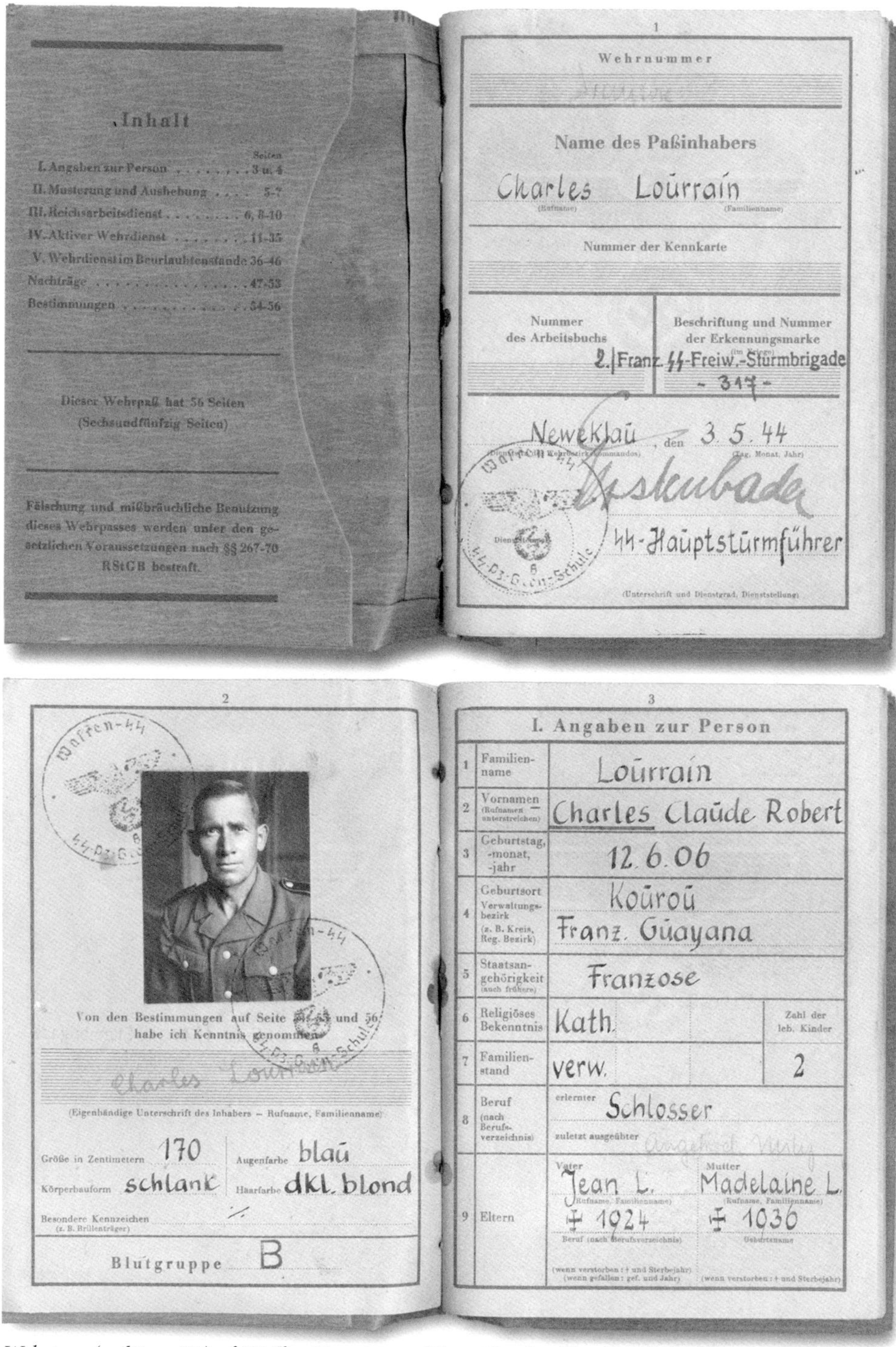

Inhalt

	Seiten
I. Angaben zur Person	3 u. 4
II. Musterung und Aushebung	5-7
III. Reichsarbeitsdienst	6, 8-10
IV. Aktiver Wehrdienst	11-35
V. Wehrdienst im Beurlaubtenstande	36-46
Nachträge	47-53
Bestimmungen	54-56

Dieser Wehrpaß hat 56 Seiten (Sechsundfünfzig Seiten)

Fälschung und mißbräuchliche Benutzung dieses Wehrpasses werden unter den gesetzlichen Voraussetzungen nach §§ 267-70 RStGB bestraft.

1

Wehrnummer

Name des Paßinhabers

Charles Lourrain

(Rufname) (Familienname)

Nummer der Kennkarte

Nummer des Arbeitsbuchs

Beschriftung und Nummer der Erkennungsmarke (im Kriege)

2./Franz. SS-Freiw.-Sturmbrigade - 317 -

Neweklau, den 3. 5. 44

(Tag, Monat, Jahr)

SS-Hauptsturmführer

(Unterschrift und Dienstgrad, Dienststellung)

2

Von den Bestimmungen auf Seite 54-56 und 56 habe ich Kenntnis genommen

Charles Lourrain

(Eigenhändige Unterschrift des Inhabers – Rufname, Familienname)

Größe in Zentimetern 170 Augenfarbe blau

Körperbauform schlank Haarfarbe dkl. blond

Besondere Kennzeichen (z. B. Brillenträger) -/-

Blutgruppe B

3

I. Angaben zur Person

1	Familienname	Lourrain
2	Vornamen (Rufnamen unterstreichen)	Charles Claude Robert
3	Geburtstag, -monat, -jahr	12. 6. 06
4	Geburtsort, Verwaltungsbezirk (z. B. Kreis, Reg. Bezirk)	Kourou, Franz. Guayana
5	Staatsangehörigkeit (auch frühere)	Franzose
6	Religiöses Bekenntnis	Kath. — Zahl der leb. Kinder: 2
7	Familienstand	verw.
8	Beruf (nach Berufsverzeichnis)	erlernter: Schlosser; zuletzt ausgeübter:
9	Eltern	Vater: Jean L. † 1924; Mutter: Madelaine L. † 1036

Wehrpass (military ID) of *Waffen-Hauptsturmführer* Charles Claude Robert Lourrain of the 2nd Company of the French SS Volunteer Assault Brigade.

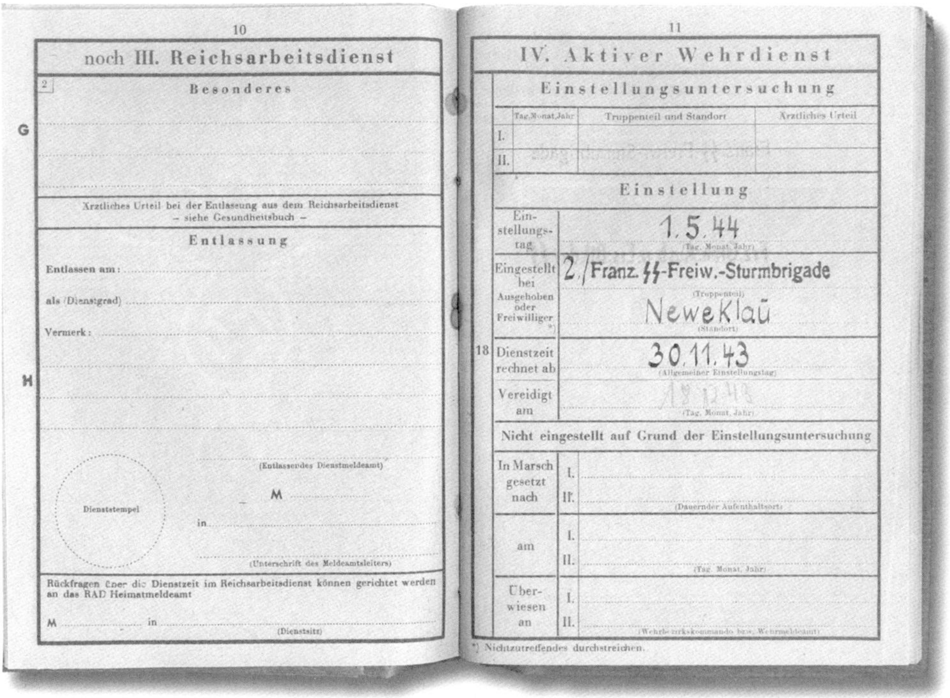

10

noch III. Reichsarbeitsdienst

2 **Besonderes**

G

Ärztliches Urteil bei der Entlassung aus dem Reichsarbeitsdienst – siehe Gesundheitsbuch –

Entlassung

Entlassen am:

als (Dienstgrad)

Vermerk:

H

(Entlassendes Dienstmeldeamt)

Dienststempel

M

in

(Unterschrift des Meldeamtsleiters)

Rückfragen über die Dienstzeit im Reichsarbeitsdienst können gerichtet werden an das RAD Heimatmeldeamt

M in (Dienstsitz)

11

IV. Aktiver Wehrdienst

Einstellungsuntersuchung

	Tag, Monat, Jahr	Truppenteil und Standort	Ärztliches Urteil
I.			
II.			

Einstellung

18

Einstellungstag	1.5.44 (Tag, Monat, Jahr)
Eingestellt bei / Ausgehoben oder Freiwilliger*)	2./Franz. SS-Freiw.-Sturmbrigade (Truppenteil) Neweklau (Standort)
Dienstzeit rechnet ab	30.11.43 (Allgemeiner Einstellungstag)
Vereidigt am	1.12.43 (Tag, Monat, Jahr)

Nicht eingestellt auf Grund der Einstellungsuntersuchung

In Marsch gesetzt nach	I. / II.	(Dauernder Aufenthaltsort)
am	I. / II.	(Tag, Monat, Jahr)
Überwiesen an	I. / II.	(Wehrbezirkskommando bzw. Wehrmeldeamt)

*) Nichtzutreffendes durchstreichen.

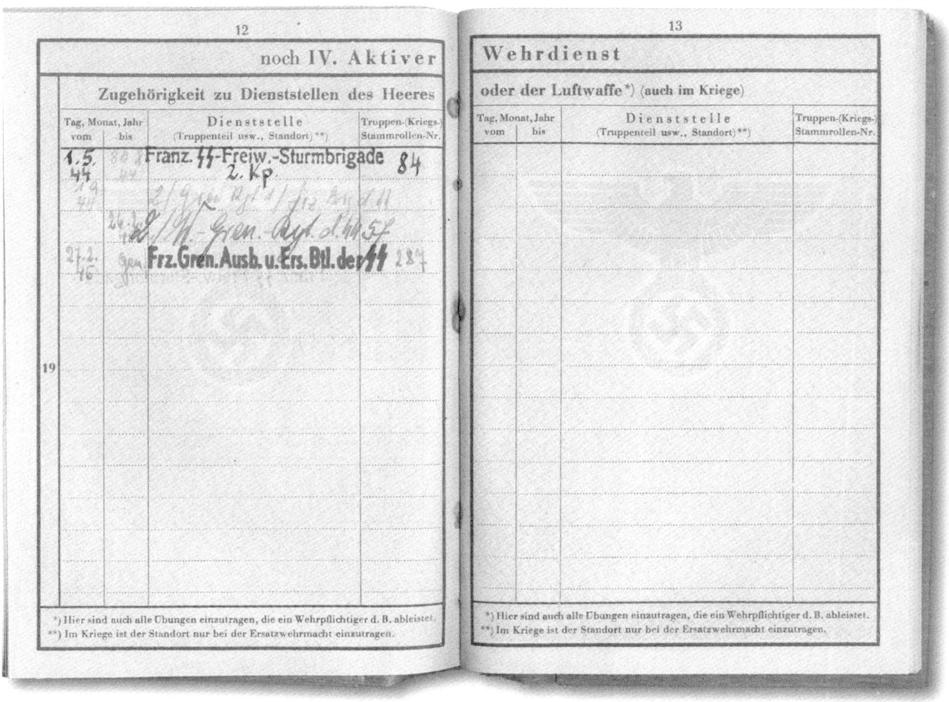

12

noch IV. Aktiver

Zugehörigkeit zu Dienststellen des Heeres

19

Tag, Monat, Jahr vom	bis	Dienststelle (Truppenteil usw., Standort)**)	Truppen-(Kriegs-) Stammrollen-Nr.
1.5.44	30.8.44	Franz. SS-Freiw.-Sturmbrigade 2. Kp.	84
1.9.44		2/Gren. Rgt. 1/Frz. Brig. d. SS [illegible]	
26.[illegible].44		2./W.-Gren.-Rgt. d. SS 57	
27.2.45	gen.	Frz. Gren. Ausb. u. Ers. Btl. der SS	287

*) Hier sind auch alle Übungen einzutragen, die ein Wehrpflichtiger d. B. ableistet.
**) Im Kriege ist der Standort nur bei der Ersatzwehrmacht einzutragen.

13

Wehrdienst

oder der Luftwaffe*) (auch im Kriege)

Tag, Monat, Jahr vom	bis	Dienststelle (Truppenteil usw., Standort)**)	Truppen-(Kriegs-) Stammrollen-Nr.

*) Hier sind auch alle Übungen einzutragen, die ein Wehrpflichtiger d. B. ableistet.
**) Im Kriege ist der Standort nur bei der Ersatzwehrmacht einzutragen.

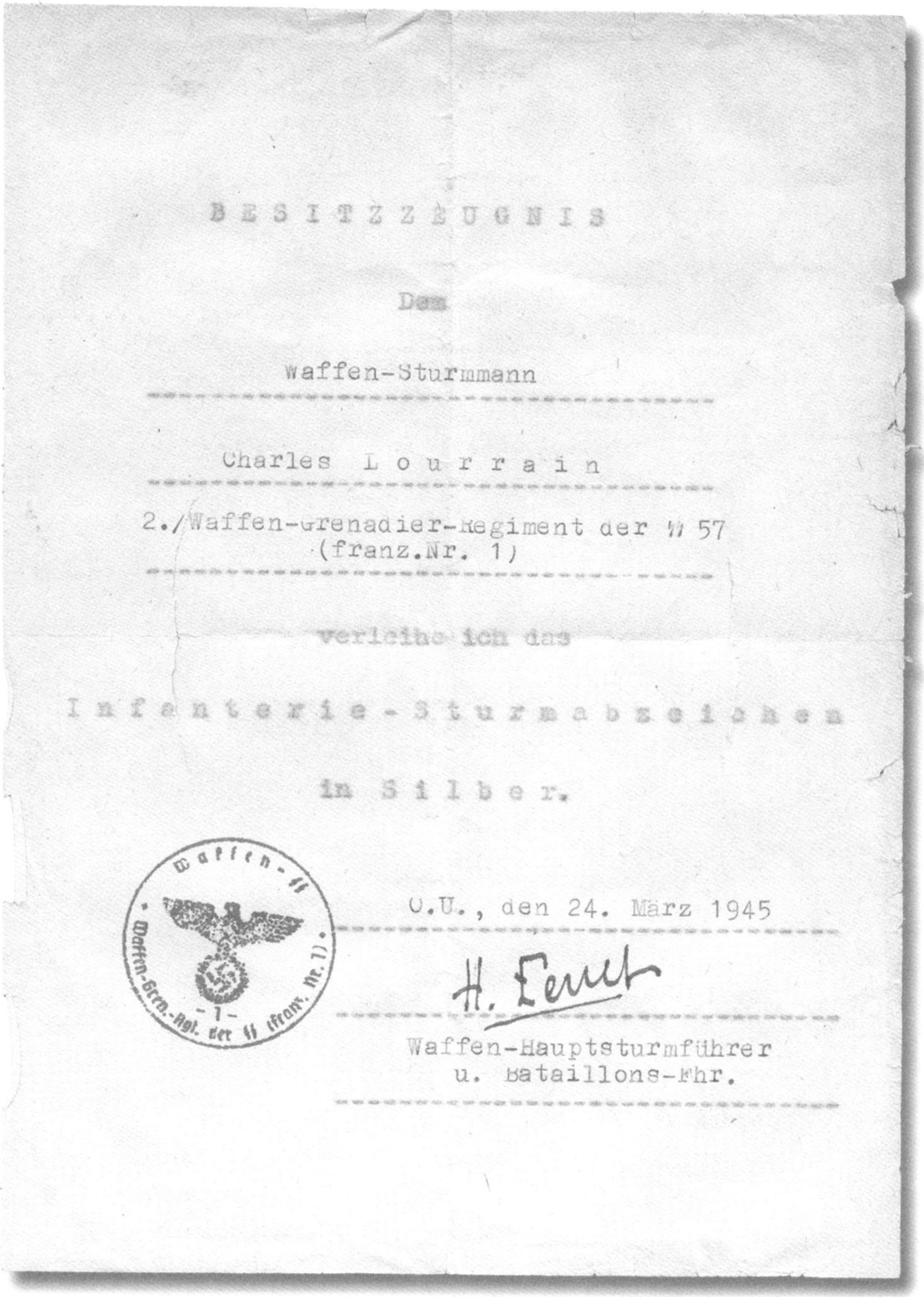

BESITZZEUGNIS

Dem

Waffen-Sturmmann

Charles Lourrain

2./Waffen-Grenadier-Regiment der SS 57
(franz.Nr. 1)

verleihe ich das

Infanterie-Sturmabzeichen

in Silber.

O.U., den 24. März 1945

H. Fenet

Waffen-Hauptsturmführer
u. Bataillons-Fhr.

Waffen-SS
Waffen-Gren.-Rgt. der SS (franz. Nr. 1)
- 1 -

On March 24, 1945, Henri Fenet awarded *Waffen-Hauptsturmführer* Lourrain the Infantry Assault Badge in Silver.

B e s i t z z e u g n i s

Dem

Waffen-Sturmmann

Charles L o u r r a i n

Gen.Kp./Frz.Gren.Ausb.u.Ers.Btl. der SS

ist auf Grund

seiner am 26.2.45 erlittenen

einmaligen Verwundung/Beschädigung

das

V E R W U N D E T E N A B Z E I C H E N

in S c h w a r z

verliehen worden.

Wildflecken,den 29.3.45

SS-Obersturmbannführer

und Bataillonskommandeur.

Award document for the Wound Badge in Black, which *Waffen-Hauptsturmführer* Lourrain received for wounds suffered during the fighting for Bärenwalde.

The *33. Waffen-Grenadier-Division der SS "Charlemagne" (französische Nr. 1)*

On February 10, 1945, Hitler ordered that the grenadier brigade, with a strength of about 7,500 men, be renamed the *33. Waffen-Grenadier-Division der SS "Charlemagne" (französische Nr. 1)*. Organized as an *Infanterie-Division 45*, nothing changed about the units' relationship to the brigade. Even the renumbering of the brigade units from 57 to 33 was not carried out. The unit received neither personnel nor materiel, and only its title changed.

When the rushed transfer order to the collapsing eastern front arrived a few days later, the positions in the new division were occupied as follows:

Division Headquarters	Military Postal Code 47 335
Commander	*Waffen-Oberführer* Puaud
1st Aide-de-Camp	*Waffen-Obersturmführer* Auphan
2nd Aide-de-Camp	*Waffen-Standartenjunker* Platon
Ia (1st General Staff Officer)	*Waffen-Sturmbannführer* de Vaugelas
Ic (3rd General Staff Officer)	*Waffen-Obersturmführer* Delile
IIa/b (Personnel Office)	*Waffen-Obersturmführer* Bénétoux
IVb (Medical Section)	*Waffen-Sturmbannführer* Dr. Lelongt
IVc (Veterinary Section)	*Waffen-Hauptsturmführer* Dr. Richert
IVd (Chaplain)	*Waffen-Sturmbannführer* de Mayol de Lupé
VI (Ideology)	*SS-Untersturmführer* Dr. Beuler
Guard and Training Company	*SS-Obersturmführer* Weber

SS-Feldgend.-Trupp 57

(Military Police Troop)	Military Postal Code 06 953
Officer	*Waffen-Obersturmführer* Veyrieras

Inspectorate of French SS Units
Military Postal Code

Commander	*SS-Brigadeführer* Dr. Krukenberg
1st Aide-de-Camp	*SS-Untersturmführer* Patzak
2nd Aide-de-Camp	*SS-Untersturmführer* Hegewald
Ia (1st General Staff Officer)	*SS-Hauptsturmführer* Jauss
Ib (2nd general Staff Officer)	*SS-Obersturmführer* Meier
Ic (3rd General Staff Officer)	*SS-Hauptsturmführer* Schmidt
IIa/b (Personnel Office)	*SS-Hauptsturmführer* Pachur
IVa (Administration)	*SS-Hauptsturmführer* Hagen
IVb (Medical Section)	*SS-Sturmbannführer* Dr. Schlegel
IVc (Veterinary Section)	*SS-Hauptsturmführer* Dr. Schreiner
V (Motor Vehicle Section)	*SS-Untersturmführer* Neubauer
VI (Ideology)	*SS-Obersturmführer* Dr. Kopp
Liaison Officers:	*SS-Sturmbannführer* Dr. von Lölhöffel
	Waffen-Hauptsturmführer Renault

Waffen-Grenadier-Regiment der SS 57 (franz. Nr. 1)
Military Postal Code 66 641

Commander	*Waffen-Hauptsturmführer* de Bourmont
Adjutant	*Waffen-Untersturmführer* Artus
Aide-de-Camp	*Waffen-Untersturmführer* Martres
Headquarters Company	*Waffen-Obersturmführer* André
13th (Infantry Gun) Company	*Waffen-Hauptsturmführer* Roy
14th (Anti-Tank) Company	*Waffen-Obersturmführer* Labuze

I. Bataillon	Military Postal Code 41 592
Commander	*Waffen-Obersturmführer* Fenet
1st Company	*Waffen-Untersturmführer* Brazier
2nd Company	*Waffen-Obersturmführer* Bartoloméi
3rd Company	*Waffen-Untersturmführer* Counil
4th Company	*Waffen-Oberscharführer* Couvreur

II. Bataillon	Military Postal Code 35 411
Commander	*Waffen-Hauptsturmführer* Obitz
5th Company	*Waffen-Oberscharführer* Hennecart
6th Company	*Waffen-Unterscharführer* Albert
7th Company	*Waffen-Standartenoberjunker* Million-Rousseau
8th Company	*Waffen-Untersturmführer* Colnion

Waffen-Grenadier-Regiment der SS 57 (franz. Nr. 2)

Military Postal Code 02 951

Commander	*Waffen-Sturmbannführer* Raybaud
Adjutant	*Waffen-Obersturmführer* Baudouin
Headquarters Company	*Waffen-Hauptsturmführer* de Perricot
13th (Infantry Gun) Company	*Waffen-Obersturmführer* Francais
14th (Anti-Tank) Company	*Waffen-Oberscharführer* Girard

I. Bataillon	Military Postal Code 03 865
Commander	*Waffen-Hauptsturmführer* Monneuse
1st Company	*Waffen-Obersturmführer* Fantin
2nd Company	*Waffen-Obersturmführer* Géromini
3rd Company	*Waffen-Untersturmführer* Rigeade
4th Company	*Waffen-Obersturmführer* Tardan

II. Bataillon	Military Postal Code 05 492
Commander	*Waffen-Sturmbannführer* Berret
5th Company	*Waffen-Hauptscharführer* Walter
6th Company	*Waffen-Obersturmführer* Louis
7th Company	*Waffen-Obersturmführer* Wagner
8th Company	*Waffen-Obersturmführer* Defever

SS-Panzerjäger-Abt. 57	Military Postal Code 66 885
Commander	*Waffen-Sturmbannführer* Boudet-Gheusi
1st (Heavy Anti-Tank Gun) Company	*Waffen-Standartenoberjunker* Vincenot
2nd (Assault Gun) Company	*Waffen-Obersturmführer* Michel
3rd (Flak) Company	*Waffen-Untersturmführer* Fayard

SS-Artillerie-Abteilung 57	Military Postal Code 00 290
Commander	*Waffen-Hauptsturmführer* Havette
1st Battery	*Waffen-Obersturmführer* Chaufour
2nd Battery	*Waffen-Obersturmführer* Salle
3rd Battery	*Waffen-Oberscharführer* Merméjean

SS-Nachrichten-Kp. 57

(Signals Company)	Military Postal Code 14 309
Commander	*Waffen-Obersturmführer* Dupuyau

SS-Pionier-Kp. 57	Military Postal Code 64 680
Commander de Vitrolles	*Waffen-Obersturmführer* Audibert

SS-Versorgungstruppen 57 (Supply)	Military Postal Code 13 630
Motor Transport Column A	*Waffen-Hauptsturmführer* Schlisler
Motor Transport Column B	*Waffen-Hauptsturmführer* Croisille
SS Workshop Company 57	*SS-Obersturmführer* Maud'huit

SS-Veterinär-Kompanie 57	Military Postal Code 11 498
Commander	*Waffen-Untersturmführer* Richter

SS-Feldpostamt 57 (Post Office)	Military Postal Code 11 498

SS-Feldersatz-Bataillon 57

(Replacement Unit)	Military Postal Code 65 920
Commander	*Waffen-Hauptsturmführer* Biziau
1st Trained Recruit Company	*Waffen-Untersturmführer* Pignard-Berthet
2nd Trained Recruit Company	*Waffen-Hauptsturmführer* Flamand
3rd Trained Recruit Company	*Waffen-Obersturmführer* de Brégaud

Französische Grenadier-Ausbildungs- und Ersatz-Bataillon der SS

(French SS Grenadier Training and Replacement Battalion)

Military Postal Code 46 765

Commander	*SS-Obersturmbannführer* Hersche
Core Company	*SS-Obersturmführer* Allgeier
Recruit Company	*Waffen-Obersturmführer* Crespin
Training Company	*SS-Untersturmführer* Schüler

The position list shows how many ranks were missing when the division went into action. In one case a *Waffen-Hauptsturmführer* (captain) commanded a regiment and a *Waffen-Obersturmführer* (lieutenant, Henri Fenet was not promoted to *Waffen-Hauptsturmführer* until March 1, 1945) a battalion. In some cases noncommissioned officers led companies. By comparison: in 1939 almost all of the platoon leaders in the *SS-Heimwehr Danzig* were SS-*Untersturmführer*.[22]

Action in Pomerania

About four months after concluding its successful summer offensive, on January 12, 1945, the Red Army launched its spring offensive. The 1st Ukrainian Front (Marshall Konev) attacked from the Baranov bridgehead, striking at the seam between the *4. Panzer-Armee* and the *17. Armee*, and by the evening of that day it had gained about twenty kilometers in the direction of Litzmannstadt. On January 13, 1945, the *Wehrmacht* communiqué noted:

> The long-awaited winter offensive by the Bolsheviks on the Vistula front has begun. After unusually powerful artillery preparation, the enemy first struck the western front of the Baranov bridgehead with numerous rifle divisions and armored units. Fierce fighting had broken out.

On the same day, the 3rd White Russian Front (Marshal Chernyakovsky) launched its offensive from Lithuania against the *3. Panzer-Armee* and *4. Armee* in East Prussia. January 14, also brought attacks by the 2nd White Russian Front (Marshal Rokossovsky) from the Narev bridgeheads in the direction of Elbing against the *2. Armee*, and by the 1st White Russian Front (Marshal Zhukov) south of Warsaw from the Magnuszew and Pulawy bridgehead in the direction of Posen against the *4. Armee* and *9. Armee*.

Although the German forces had exploited every possible advantage to meet the coming big attack by the Red Army, outnumbered ten to one in personnel and equipment, they could do little. With massed air and artillery support, the enemy broke through the in-depth defense lines. In the end the enemy forces advanced faster than the German units, lacking fuel for their vehicles and heavy weapons, could retreat. With the exception of those in so-called fortresses, for example Posen and Schneidemühl, which were set up for all-round defense around strategically important communications junctions, a move that was supposed to prevent the Soviets from using the railroads, many German units were simply overrun.[23] On January 17, 1945, the Wehrmacht clockwork mechanism reported:

> The situation in the large bend of the Vistula has become critical. The enemy has thrown ninety rifle divisions and fifteen tank corps into the battle there. In heavy fighting, enemy armored spearheads have advanced as far as the area north of Cracow, into the Tschenstochau area, southwest of Tomaschow and northwest of Warsaw. Behind the enemy spearheads, powerful German battle groups are putting up fierce resistance against the following Bolshevik units. Panzer divisions fought a sacrificial action in the Kielce area, preventing an enemy breakthrough for two days and allowing our troops to withdraw from the Vistula front.

The Red Army drove into areas almost devoid of German troops and the terrified civilian populations fled frantically in conditions of ice and snow. Within two weeks the remaining parts of the Generalgouvernement still in German hands and the Wartheland District had been lost. The enemy was at the Oder in the west and the Frische Haff in the north near Elbing. The encirclement of the *3. Panzer-Armee* and the *4. Armee* in East Prussia was just a matter of time.

The Soviet forces had smashed Army Groups Center and A even more quickly than in the summer of 1944 and had gained another 400 kilometers of ground towards the west. The rapid advance to the west and northwest had created a gap of several hundred kilometers between the *2. Armee* in West Prussia and the *9. Armee* in Silesia. Hitler reacted to this by forming a new army group on January 21, 1945.

The next day *Generaloberst* Guderian, chief of the army general staff, learned of Hitler's decision by telex:[24]

> 1.) By order of the *Führer*, the *Reichsführer-SS* is assuming command of Army group Vistula now being formed.
> 2.) His mission is:
>   a) To close the gap between Army Groups A and Center, prevent the enemy from breaking through in the direction of Posen and Danzig and thus prevent East Prussia from being cut off and to guard the deployment of fresh forces.
>   b) To organize the national defense behind the entire Eastern Front on German soil.
>   c) Troops:

Attached to Army Group Vistula will be:

a) *9. Armee* (with all army units), (timing to be determined)
b) *2. Armee* (with all army units),
c) 300 tank-killing teams (to be provided by the generals of anti-tank defense of all branches),
d) Defense Districts 2, 3, 20 and 21 including *Gneisenau* and *Volkssturm* units to be formed in those defense districts,
e) Orders for further attachments to follow.

4.) Borders (1:1 million map):
   a) To the right to Army Group A (later Center): Fortress Glogau–Krotoschin–Ostrowo–Petrikau (towns on the Vistula),
   b) To the left to Army Group Center (later North): Elbing (Vistula)–Osterode (Center)–Willenberg (Center)

5.) Army Group Vistula to report timing of readiness to work and possible assumption of command.

6.) The Headquarters of Army Group Vistula are being formed from the Waffen-SS and army with more detailed direction from the *Reichsführer-SS*. The organizational department to settle details directly with the *Reichsführer-SS*.
Quartermaster-General to set up senior quartermaster staff in direct consultation with the *Reichsführer-SS* and regulate the provision of necessary transport capacity.

7.) Chief of Army Signals will direct the provision of signals units.

8.) Headquarters: Schneidemühl.

On January 21, 1945, *Reichsführer-SS* Himmler gave up his previous command of Army Group Upper Rhine to *SS-Oberstgruppenführer* Hausser and travelled in his special train Steiermark (Styria) to Marienburg (southeast of Dirschau). There he delivered one of his typically pathetic speeches to political and military leaders. Dr. Hans Leeser, the former mayor of the city of Elbing in West Prussia, remembered:[25]

> On Sunday evening, January 21, 1945, the Volkssturm's district headquarters leader, the well-known Knight's Cross wearer and U-boat commander *Kapitän zur See* Hartmann, telephoned and told me that there was no reason for any unrest among the population of Elbing, as there was going to be a fundamental change in the military situation in a few days.

> He had just come from a meeting in Marienburg, where *Reichsführer-SS* Himmler had declared that he had been named commander of the new Army Group Vistula and that everything would be returned to order in a few days.
>
> On the side I would like to note the following: In the spring of 1946, I was with the former *Gauleiter* Forster[26] for a short time in the Fallingbostel interment camp. I asked him about the meeting with Himmler in Marienburg. He told me the following:
>
> Himmler lied to us terribly. He moved tank armies around on a big map, giving us the impression that the situation would soon change. Afterwards it turned out that these panzer armies weren't even present.

Simultaneously began the mobilization of the alert units that had been formed when the codeword *Gneisenau* was issued on January 13, 1945. These were units of the replacement army in which most of the recruits were supposed to have had at least four weeks of training. Among them were sixteen- and seventeen-year-olds who had just been issued their uniforms.

When the Soviet offensive began, the front held by the *2. Armee*—to which the Frenchmen were to be attached in mid-February 1945—followed a line Novogród (about twelve kilometers west of Lomza) from the mouth of the Pisa River, along the Narev through Ostrolenka and Rózan to Ostenburg (Polish Pultusk) and from there along the road to Nasielsk in the area east of Modlin. By January 18, 1945, the 2. Armee had to pull back to the line Praschnitz (Polish Przasnysz)–Mielau (Polish Mlawa)–Strzegowo–Plöhnen (Polish Plonsk)–Hohenburg (Polish Wyszogród). Cohesion within the army could barely be maintained because of the powerful advances made by the Red Army.

On January 30, 1945, Himmler announced his directive for the conduct of operations in the following days to the units under his command (Headquarters, *9. Armee*, Headquarters, *2. Armee* and the acting Headquarters, *Armee-Korps*):[27]

> 1. The army group's first priority is to use all available means to prevent a further westward advance by the enemy. As a result, greater importance is attached to the holding of even minor strongpoints, to split the enemy advance. Only under these conditions can the army group correctly employ the large formations which are on their way.

2. To this end, *9. Armee* is to defend to the end the Lissa–Oder Corner line on its right wing and the Oder–Warthe position. Groups of tanks that break through are to be hunted down and destroyed by assault guns and tank-killing squads. The corner post of Landsberg is to be reinforced. The enemy must be prevented from breaking through towards Küstrin. In the gap between the *V. SS-* and *X. SS-Korps*, enemy armored units that have broken through are to be attacked and destroyed by the *Panzergruppe* where they are met. Maximum boldness and mobility are the order of the day. On the army's northern wing, the breakwater of Schneidemühl, in particular, is to be held. Reinforcing the security garrison in the Pomerania position is important in this sector.
3. The focus of the defense in the *2. Armee*'s sector remains its two wings. On its southern front the army must wage mobile warfare to prevent a further breakthrough to the northwest. The 32nd Division is to be used to create the conditions for the firming up of this sector. Breakout by the garrison of Fortress Thorn by special verbal order.

Himmler's pithy sayings ignored the reality of the situation. On February 9, 1945, the *2. Armee*'s main line of resistance began at the Frische Haff and ran through the Nogat to Marienburg. The army's attempts to restore contact with the *4. Armee* east of Elbing were frustrated by Soviet fire. At the front, the troops of Acting Headquarters *XX. Armee-Korps* (Danzig) were committed against the Soviet 2nd Shock Army. To the south, along the Vistula, was the *XXIII. Armee-Korps*, which bordered the *XXVII. Armee-Korps* with a bridgehead near Graudenz. This corps area, which was opposite the Soviet 65th Army, arced through Schwetz to Osche, which was in the area of the *XXXXVI. Panzer-Korps*. Facing it was the Soviet 49th Army. The main line of resistance then continued west through Pruszcz to Landeck. There, on the extreme right wing of the *2. Armee*, was the *XVI. SS-Armee-Korps*, which was attempting to maintain contact with the *11. Armee*. Near Pruszcz the Soviet 70th Army launched repeated offensives in an attempt to break through between the *XVI. SS-* and *XXXXVI. Panzer-Korps*.

The situation was deteriorating by the hour. In the search for troops with which to somehow "plug" the gap in the front, attention also fell on the *33. SS Waffen Grenadier Division der SS "Charlemagne,"* then being formed in Wildflecken. On February 15, 1945, the day the division was placed on alert, Army Group Vistula reported the *2. Armee*'s situation to the Army High Command:

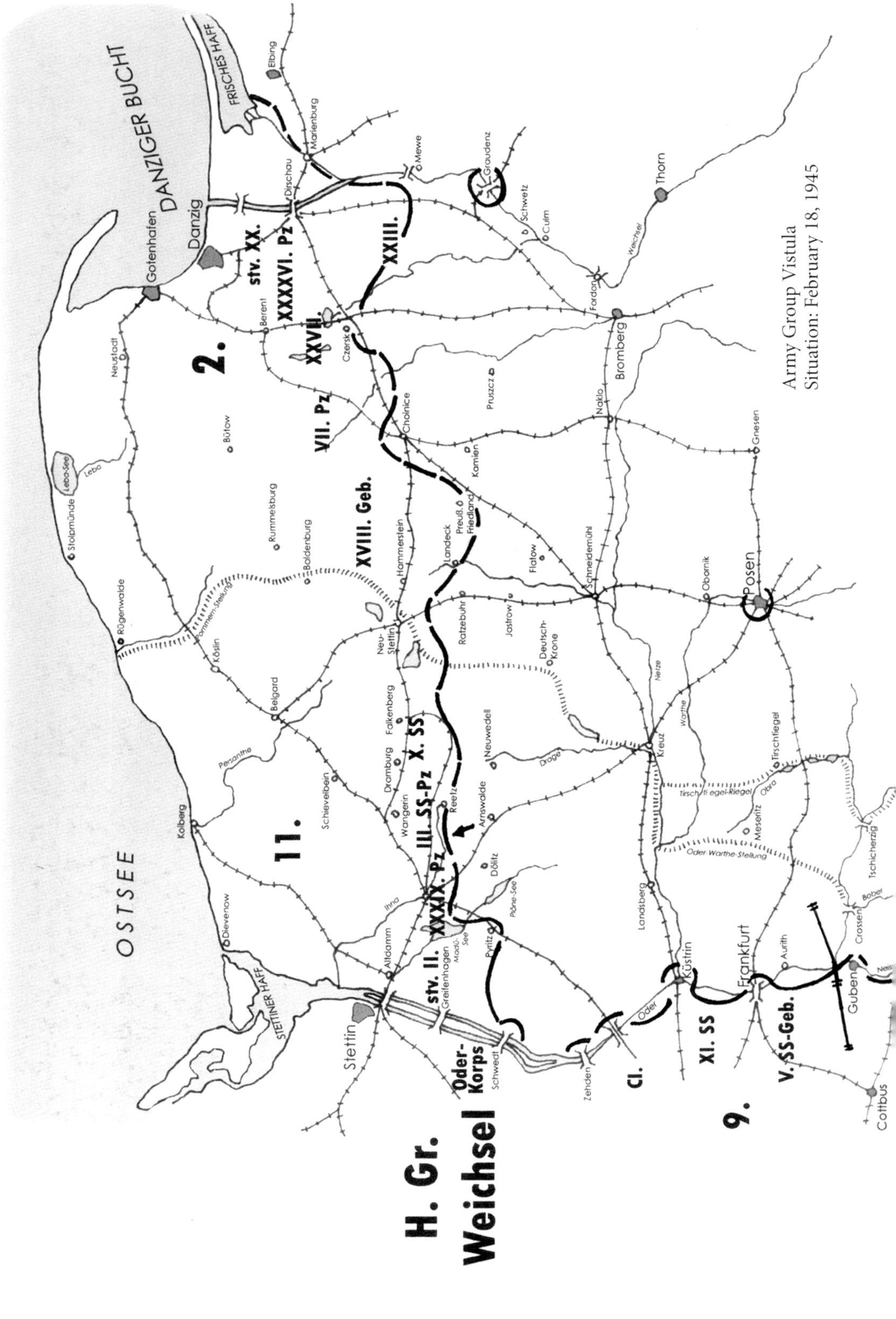

Army Group Vistula
Situation: February 18, 1945

Today the situation on the army group's left wing became more critical. The enemy expanded his attacks into the Pr.-Friedland area and attempted with some success to break through the flanking barrier in the area south of Konitz by attacking from all sides, in order to create the conditions for a strategic breakthrough to the north and northeast. At the same time, employing powerful forces he continued his attacks against the *2. Armee*'s southern front on either side of Tuchel, and achieved significant penetrations in the difficult terrain of the Tucheler Heide, which allowed him to insert forces without being detected. The army has no forces with which to seal off or eliminate these. [...]

The fighting strength of our units, which have been in the fiercest combat in this sector of the front for days, has been considerably weakened. This is especially true of the two panzer divisions (*4.* and *7. Pz.Div.*), which are bearing the main burden of the fighting in the area around Konitz. They have a combined total of just thirty-six serviceable tanks and twelve assault guns.

If the enemy succeeds in forcing the *XXXXVI. Panzer-Korps* further into the Tucheler Heide, which at present cannot be prevented with the forces available, there is danger that the enemy will split the *2. Armee* and bring about the collapse of the Vistula front. [...]

According to statements by prisoners, here (west of the Vistula) the enemy is massing elements of the 2nd Shock Army west of Graudenz for an attack on February 16, 1945, to cut off and isolate the corner post of Graudenz.

The first units of the *33. SS Waffen Grenadier Division der SS "Charlemagne"* began entraining at Wildflecken Station two days later. According to the appendices of the war diary of Army Group Vistula, the following were sent to the *XVIII. Gebirgs-Korps* in Rummelsburg:

2 grenadier regiments each with 2 battalions
2 light infantry gun companies
1 artillery battalion with two batteries, each with 4 light field howitzers
2 Panzerschreck companies
1 37 mm flak company
1 mixed signals company
1 field post office
1 first-aid company

In Pomerania the French volunteers were issued seventy-two Panzerschreck anti-tank weapons.

1 ambulance platoon
1 veterinary company
1 military police company
1 workshop platoon

Altogether this force consisted of 102 officers, 886 noncommissioned officers and 5,375 enlisted men (6,363 men of all ranks). They had the following weapons and equipment:

3,643 carbines
1,030 pistols
30 MG42 heavy machine-guns
3 50 mm light anti-tank guns
12 75 mm infantry guns
8 105 mm field howitzers
3 prime movers
1,082 horses
72 *panzerschreck*
538 submachine-guns
66 MG43 light machine-guns
31 MG34
3 75 mm heavy anti-tank guns
9 37 mm anti-aircraft guns
44 trucks
3 *Raupenschlepper Ost* tractors
872 *panzerfausts*

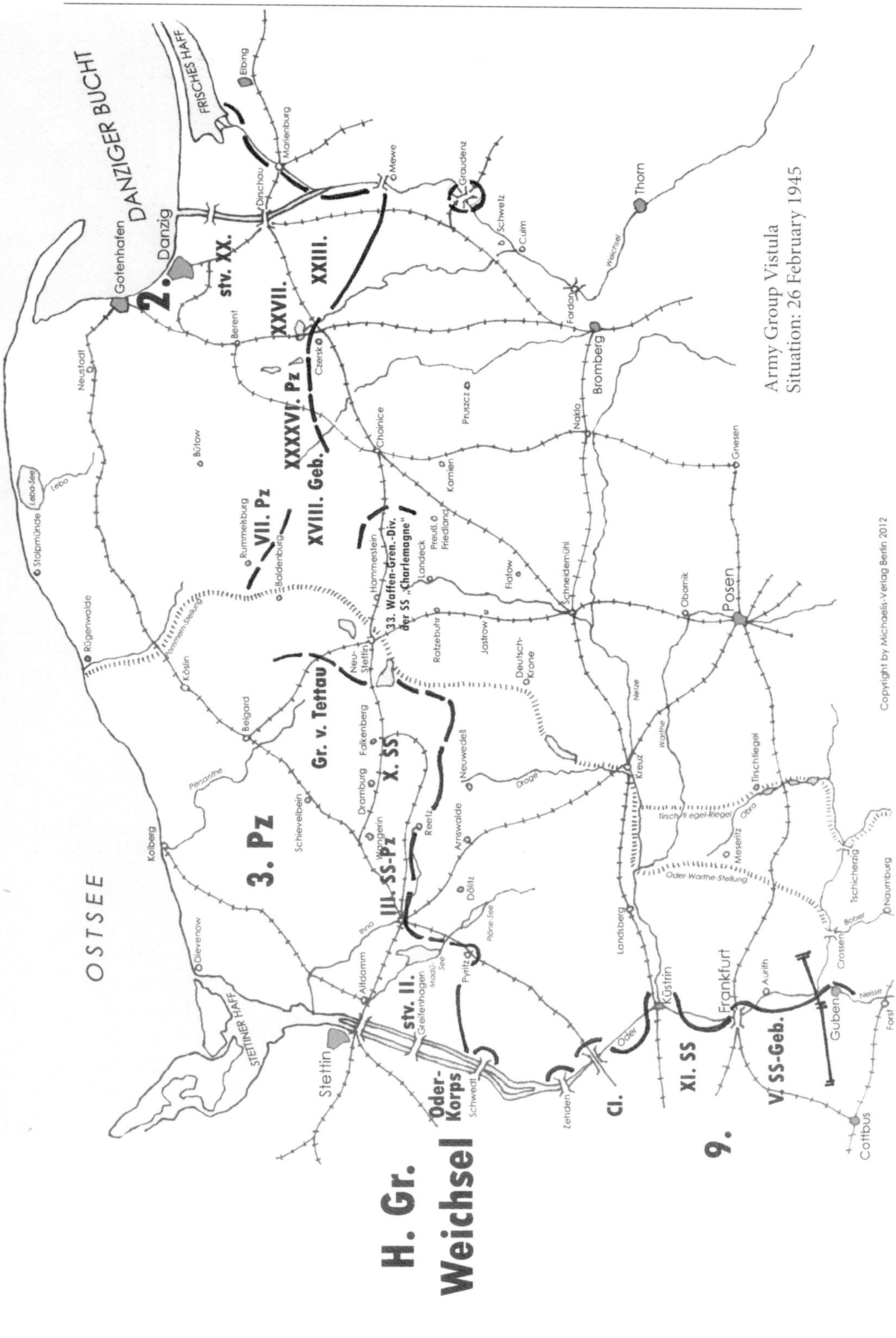

Army Group Vistula
Situation: 26 February 1945

Thus each soldier did not even have his own weapon. In addition to these just under 6,400 soldiers, *SS-Feldersatz-Bataillon 57* with about 600 men was still in Greifenberg as was the *Französische SS-Grenadier-Ausbildungs- und Ersatz-Bataillon der SS* with about 900 troops.

With the Red Army in the area southeast of Hammerstein making preparations for a breakthrough to the Baltic Sea, the trains carrying the French units to Rummelsburg were rerouted to Hammerstein. The first eighteen trains, carrying about 450 men, arrived at the railway station there at about two in the morning on February 22, 1945. They were the 1st, 3rd and 4th Companies of *Waffen-Grenadier-Regiment der SS 57 (französische Nr. 1)*, which were proceeding to Training Camp Hammerstein at the disposal of the *2. Armee*.

The next night Soviet tanks advanced towards Schlochau (approximately twenty kilometers east of Hammerstein), intending to reach the Baltic via Baldenburg (approximately thirty kilometers north of Hammerstein). The three companies were alerted and placed under the command of *General der Infanterie* Hochbaum, commanding general of the *XVIII. Gebirgs-Korps*. At about noon on February 23, 1945, he ordered troops into the area southeast of Hammerstein. While the first French SS volunteers had already left the training camp, the second troop transport arrived in Wildflecken during the night of February 24. It also carried approximately 450 troops (2nd Company and the first elements of *II./Waffen-Grenadier-Regiment der SS 57*). The men were immediately moved to the front and together with the three companies from the first transport were attached to the *32. Infanterie-Division*. It deployed the French soldiers on the division's right wing next to the *15. Waffen-Grenadier-Division der SS (lettische Nr. 1)*.

Then, at about noon on February 24, 1945, the *I. Bataillon* (*Waffen-Obersturmführer* Fenet) was ordered to occupy positions around Heinrichswalde and the *II. Bataillon* (*Waffen-Hauptsturmführer* Obitz) near Barkenfelde (approximately four kilometers east of Heinrichswalde. Both villages were in fact already in enemy hands. Costly attempts to take them produced only short-lived success. After enemy tank units were able to break through the lines of the *15. Waffen-Grenadier-Division der SS (lettische Nr. 1)* to the north in the Peterswalde (approximately eight kilometers southwest of Barkenfelde)–Schönwerder area, *Waffen-Grenadier-Regiment der SS 57* (*Waffen-Hauptsturmführer* de Bourmont) withdrew into the Bärenwalde area approximately four kilometers to the north.

The landscape in the Heinrichswalde–Bärenwalde–Elsenau area.

The cemetery in Heinrichswalde.

Roads and rail lines in the Heinrichswalde–Bärenwalde–Elsenau area.

The railroad station in Bärenwalde.

The *I. Bataillon* of *Waffen-Grenadier-Regiment der SS 57 (französische Nr. 2)* under the command of *Waffen-Hauptsturmführer* Monneuse had meanwhile also moved into position there on the morning of February 26, 1945. Contact between the three French battalions and the units on their left (*32. Infanterie-Division*) and right (*15. Waffen-Grenadier-Division der SS*) was very tentative. Despite a vigorous defense, the French battalions were split up by fierce Soviet attacks using large numbers of tanks and flamethrowers. They withdrew from Bärenwalde and the area to its west towards the small villages of Bärenhütte and Elsenau, approximately four kilometers to the north. *II./SS Waffen-Grenadier-Regiment der SS 57* was shattered in the fighting in and around Elsenau. A former French volunteer recalled the fighting at Elsenau:

> The fighting was truly bitter and the Russians advanced with great difficulty. They began combing through the cemetery. A French prisoner of war who had voluntarily joined us and the Waffen-SS was killed there. The Russians killed all the wounded who fell into their hands. Soldiers of uncertain nationality now appeared on the Russian side. They shouted insults at us in excellent French: Give up, you pack of swine!

The *II./Waffen-Grenadier-Regiment der SS 58 (französische Nr. 2)* under the command of *Waffen-Hauptsturmführer* Berret had meanwhile also assembled in Hammerstein and proceeded to Bärenhütte (approximately five kilometers east of Hammerstein), and on the afternoon of February 26, it absorbed the remnants of the regiment's *I. Bataillon* and of *II./Waffen-Grenadier-Regiment der SS* 57. Soviet troops also attacked Bärenhütte on the night of February 27 and there, too, forced the French to withdraw. The former SS volunteer André Beaurivage received his training in *SS-Pionier-Ausbildungs- und Ersatz-Bataillon 2* (SS Pioneer Training and Replacement Battalion). He recalled the move to Pomerania and the fighting at Hammerstein:

> There had been no pioneer training in Wildflecken. All of this training took place in Pikowitz. We carried out pioneer exercises, for example building bridges at the Sassau, learned how to use mines against armored vehicles, attacks on tanks and bunkers, and the use of flamethrowers and panzerfausts. Our training also included several route marches and night exercises.

The old school in Elsenau.

The village church in Elsenau.

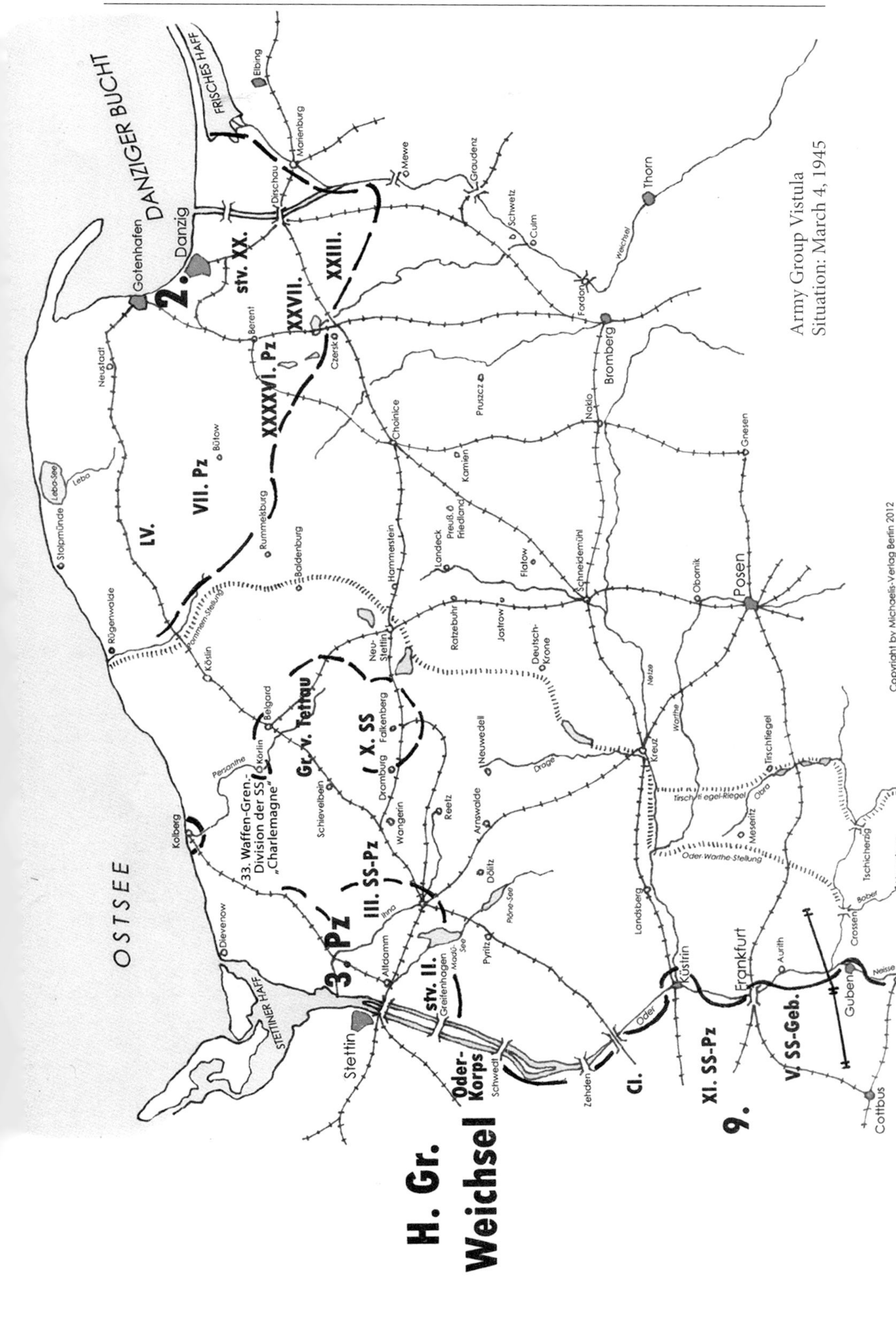

Army Group Vistula
Situation: March 4, 1945

In the second week of February 1945, we left Pikowitz for Wildflecken, where we were expected. We did not leave the rail cars and were transported very quickly. The transport was enlarged through the addition of a battery of our flak artillery. We still had no pioneer equipment, only our personal weapons we had used in training, with a very small quantity of ammunition. The anti-aircraft company also had only a few practice guns. We were supposed to get all of our equipment, brand new, in Hammerstein in Pomerania, and I actually saw the equipment at Hammerstein Station.[28]

After leaving Wildflecken we passed through Fulda, which had just been bombarded again. Apart from several brief stops along the way, we pioneers were not used to help repair the tracks, however. Not even in Fulda, where we sat for several hours. On our arrival in Hammerstein the company was immediately committed as infantry to relieve the pressure on our Latvian SS comrades, or at least what was left of them. But the Russians had already taken the position in the days previous, and we were forced to take heavy casualties while trying to move forward into the position.

The anti-aircraft battery came with us, also in the infantry role. After several hours our internal contacts were severed and we pulled back with stragglers. Sometimes there were even groups of Soviet soldiers among us.

Once I also took charge of about twenty Latvians, who were completely exhausted, physically and mentally. That was the end of our deployment in this sector. The retreat began. The pioneer and flak artillery equipment stayed at Hammerstein Station in perfect order.

I was reunited with some pioneer and flak artillery comrades in Neustrelitz, but both units no longer existed.

On February 27, 1945, what was left of the battalions plus SS Battle Group Katzian, formed from former French Kriegsmarine volunteers on February 26, withdrew towards Neustettin, approximately twenty-five kilometers to the west. There the troops were given the opportunity to rest briefly in the barracks buildings. Once again, about 500 men had been killed, wounded, reported missing or captured by the Soviets in just three days of fighting. Presumably there were some deserters as well.

During the day the artillery pieces and anti-aircraft guns of *SS-Artillerie-Abteilung 57* and *3. (Flak)/SS-Panzerjäger-Abteilung 57* arrived in Neustettin, however, they were immediately redirected to the defense of Kolberg along with gun crews.[29] When the Red Army turned toward Neustettin from the north on the morning of February 28, 1945, it triggered the hasty evacuation of the remaining civilian population and the departure of the French units.

Under the command of the aide de camp, *Waffen-Obersturmführer* Auphan, the flak battery's gun crews—whose 37 mm guns had been transported to Kolberg—and *Waffen-Grenadier-Regiment der SS* 58's anti-tank company plus the regiment's 4th Company were combined to form an approximately 250-man-strong battle group. Together with army units, it was supposed to secure the evacuation of the city. After fierce street fighting, the battle group then followed the departing troops in the direction of Belgard, about fifty-five kilometers to the northwest. They arrived there on March 1, 1945, with no further fighting.

As *Waffen-Oberführer* Puaud was physically and mentally exhausted, *SS-Brigadeführer* Krukenberg, the inspector of French SS units, took command of the elements of the *33. SS Waffen Grenadier Division der SS "Charlemagne"* that were assembling south of Belgard.

When the Red Army reached the Baltic Sea north of Köslin—between Kolberg and Rügenwalde—by way of Baldenburg and thus split Army Group Vistula in two, the bulk of the French SS unit fell under the command of Korpsgruppe von Tettau (*3. Panzer-Armee*). It gave the order to immediately occupy defensive positions to the east along the Persante near Körlin (approximately ten kilometers northwest of Belgard).

To this end the unit, which had been rushed into action and then virtually destroyed, was reorganized. For March 2, 1945, *SS-Brigadeführer* Krukenberg ordered the formation of a *Marsch-Regiment* (trained replacement regiment) from those elements fit for combat (*Waffen-Sturmbannführer* Raybaud) and a reserve regiment from the tired units, which had already lost most of their heavy weapons (*Waffen-Hauptsturmführer* de Bourmont). Both regiments had two battalions, with the first formed from *Waffen-Grenadier-Regiment der SS 57 (französische Nr. 1)* and the second from *Waffen-Grenadier-Regiment der SS 58 (französische Nr. 2)* in each case.

The trained replacement regiment arrived in the new Körlin area of operations on the morning of March 3, 1945, and it was joined by *SS-Feldersatz-Bataillon 57* (*Waffen-Hauptsturmführer* Rémy) later in the day. The latter unit consisted of three companies and had been formed from the French SS Grenadier Training and Replacement Battalion in Greifenberg on January 23, 1945. At the same time the reserve regiment also arrived in the area and secured along the Pesante north of Körlin with light infantry weapons.

SS-Feldersatz-Bataillon 57 occupied positions in Körlin, while *I./Marsch-Regiment* (*Waffen-Hauptsturmführer* Fenet) was supposed to defend the city in a southeasterly direction and *II./Marsch-Regiment* (*Waffen-Sturmbannführer* Bassompierre) in a northeasterly direction. During the night of March 4, Soviet troops (including Polish units) broke through to the north at the seam between the *III. (germanische) SS-Panzer-Korps* and the *X. SS-Armee-Korps*, advanced unopposed west past Körlin at five the next morning reached the coast near Kolberg (approximately twenty-five kilometers northwest of Körlin). As a result, the French volunteers—now attached to *Divisionsgruppe Munzel*—were cut off from the west together with elements of *Korpsgruppe von Tettau* and the *X. SS-Armee-Korps*.

When, at noon on March 4, 1945, powerful enemy groupings finally turned east in the direction of Körlin, *II./Reserve-Regiment* (*Waffen-Hauptsturmführer* Monneuse) was pulled out of its previous positions and moved into defensive positions in the area west of Körlin. The French units were thus positioned with their front facing west, south and east. *SS-Brigadeführer* Krukenberg finally decided to evacuate Körlin and initially march southeast, where it was assumed they would find German units. From there he intended to try to make contact with the German main line of resistance to the southwest.

The headquarters and *I./Marsch-Regiment* were the first to leave Körlin, during the night of March 5, 1945. The *Reserve-Regiment* (*Waffen-Hauptsturmführer* de Bourmont) followed, while *II./Marsch-Regiment*, which was acting as rearguard, had already been encircled by enemy troops in Körlin. The vanguard, under the command of *SS-Brigadeführer* Krukenberg, reached the outskirts of Belgard, in which fierce fighting was raging. It subsequently did not enter the city, instead bypassing it to the southwest. The units rested briefly in a wood near Boissin with snow falling steadily, and at 0900 marched on in the direction of Schlenzig (approximately twelve kilometers northwest of Schievelbein). Striving to remain undetected by the Red Army, the men reached the town on March 6, 1945.

Krukenberg set the next objective, Greifenberg, which was about thirty kilometers to the west. His units arrived there the next evening. As there were already strong enemy forces there, he and his men bypassed the town to the northwest. On March 9, 1945, the battalion reached the Baltic near Horst (approx. twenty kilometers east of Dievenow) and from there moved to Rewahl, about four kilometers away. After a day of rest, the French volunteers set out to break through to the German bridgehead at Dievenow.

On the morning of March 11, 1945, the men of *I./Marsch-Regiment* regained the German main line of resistance and were immediately directed to the Swinemünde area, approximately twenty-five kilometers away. From there they marched to Jargelin (approximately two kilometers north of Anklam), arriving on March 16.

The main group—essentially the *Reserve-Regiment* (*Waffen-Hauptsturmführer* de Bourmont)—including *Waffen-Oberführer* Puaud, marched out of Körlin via Belgard into the wooded area near Zarnefanz–Ristow–Boissin, approximately five kilometers south of the city. A former member remembered:

> Following a conference at 1800, *SS-Brigadeführer* Krukenberg, *SS-Standartenführer* Zimmermann and *SS-Hauptsturmführer* Jauss made their way to the *I./Marsch-Regiment,* which left its station in Redlin at the appointed hour. *Waffen-Oberführer* Puaud, however, refused to join the advance guard and declared that he intended to stay until the last man left. He gave away some of his baggage and kept only the legion flag, which he wrapped around his body beneath his uniform. At about one in the morning on March 5, 1945, he changed his mind, and decided to leave Körlin with *Waffen-Sturmbannführer* de Vaugelas and *Waffen-Hauptsturmführer* Renault in order to reach the advance guard. His vehicle broke down on the road to Belgard, however, and he was forced to march with the main body of troops (de Bourmont regiment).

They obviously used the same road as the advance guard, which led through Belgard's cemetery and thus bypassed the burning town. According to *Waffen-Oberführer* Puaud's wife, her husband was killed or was wounded and subsequently took his life[30] at the Belgard cemetery on March 6, 1945.

After the Reserve Regiment was surrounded by enemy armored forces in the wooded area, *Waffen-Hauptsturmführer* de Bourmont tried to break out towards the southwest covered by dense morning fog. As soon as the fog began to clear, Soviet tanks immediately opened fire. The main group of the *33. SS Waffen Grenadier Division der SS "Charlemagne,"* about 3,000 men strong, was gripped by panic and in a short time became completely dispersed. Most of the troops were captured by the Soviets. The number of fallen is not known; small groups tried to fight their way through west towards Greifenberg.

The *II./Marsch-Regiment,* which covered the withdrawal from Körlin, was surrounded in the town by Soviet troops on March 5, 1945. After two days of fierce fighting, on the night of March 7, battalion commander *Waffen-Hauptsturmführer* Bassompierre ordered a breakout to the southeast. In constant contact with the enemy, the companies reached Schievelbein, where they were finally scattered by the Red Army. In addition to killed and wounded—some of whom were shot when captured—the bulk of the men were captured by the Soviets, immediately or while trying to reach the Oder. Only isolated, small groups managed to reach the German main line of resistance.

Edgar Puaud wearing the Iron Cross, Second Class. When this photo was taken he was a colonel and commander of the LVF. Puaud is in French uniform.

Waffen-Oberführer Puaud with *Waffen-Hauptsturmführer* Renault during the retreat from Körlin.

Remnants of the *33. Waffen-Grenadier-Division der SS "Charlemagne"* in Pomerania, 1945.

Action in Kolberg

After Soviet tanks drove between the *III. (germanische) SS-Panzer-Korps* and the *X. SS-Armee-Korps*, reaching the Falkenberg–Dramburg area on March 1, 1945, they turned towards the *III. SS-Panzer-Korps* on the one hand, while continuing towards Kolberg on the Baltic Sea on the other.

The city, in which there were about 85,000 civilians (including about 50,000 refugees), was subsequently declared a fortress by Hitler. This had less to do with the city's strategic significance than the effort to allow the civilians to be evacuated across the Baltic. *Oberst* Fullriede was named commander of the fortress and he expressed his mission in an order of the day to the troops under his command:

> For us the defensive struggle has meaning only until the refugees and the civilian population in the city have been rescued by sea. You are all defending not this city of Kolberg, but the people living in it. That is the duty of all of us.

In addition to *SS-Artillerie-Abteilung 57* (*Waffen-Hauptsturmführer* Havette) formed at the end of February 1945 and the nine 37 mm anti-aircraft guns of *3. (Flak)/SS-Panzerjäger-Abteilung 57*, the garrison of Kolberg consisted of:

I./Feldausbildungs-Regiment des Pz.A.O.K. 3 (I Battalion/Field Training Regiment of Headquarters, 3rd Panzer Army),
Volkssturm Battalion under *SA-Standartenführer* Pfeiffer,
Festungs-MG-Bataillon 51 (Fortress Machine-gun Battalion 51)
Flak-Bataillon Heinze and a *Volkssturm* mortar platoon

Fortress Kolberg thus had a strength of about 3,300 men, which at times faced two Polish divisions. While the bulk of the French artillerymen took part in the defensive struggle with their guns, a roughly 150-man-strong battle group was formed from members of the supply train and surplus gunners.

Elements were immediately sent into the street fighting, while others were deployed outside Kolberg to bolster the main line of resistance. On March 10, 1945, French SS troops retook the cemetery near the Kolberg gas works. This enabled a number of German tanks to break through to the encircled. Ultimately they were forced to withdraw back through the outskirts into the city center again. There was heavy fighting until March 18, 1945, during which the gunners also fought as infantry after the loss of their pieces. While the fighting raged, the civilians were evacuated across the Baltic in smaller and larger vessels.

By March 18, 1945, the German lines had been reduced to a section of beach roughly 1,800 by 400 meters east of the Peresante. Among the last defenders were some French volunteers, who the next day crossed the Baltic to Swinemünde, from where they were ordered to the Wildflecken training camp. *Oberst* Fritz Fullriede had accomplished his mission and on March 23, 1945, he was awarded the 803rd Knight's Cross of the Iron Cross with Oak Leaves by Hitler.

Action in the Gotenhafen Area

During the fighting in the Elsenau–Bärenwalde–Heinrichsfelde area in late February 1945, elements of the *33. SS Waffen Grenadier Division der SS "Charlemagne"* became separated from the main body of the division. *Waffen-Hauptsturmführer* Obitz, former commander of *II./Waffen-Grenadier-Regiment der SS 57*, subsequently assumed command of these men. Following the Soviet advance in the direction of Baldenburg, the group lost contact with the division and tried to make contact with German forces east of the breakthrough. After an eighty-kilometer march towards the northeast, it finally reached Schlawe (approximately twenty kilometers south of Rügenwalde). On March 3, 1945, it unexpectedly ran into a battery of *SS-Artillerie-Abteilung 57*, which had just completed its artillery training in Josefstadt (Protectorate).

On March 5, 1945, with about 500 men, *Waffen-Hauptsturmführer* Obitz attached himself to the *4. SS-Polizei-Panzer-Grenadier-Division*, which was deployed there as part of the *VII. SS-Panzer-Korps*. The division's commander, *SS-Standartenführer* Harzer, immediately ordered the Frenchmen transferred to the Neustadt (approximately twenty-five kilometers northwest of Gotenhafen) area, roughly 100 kilometers farther to the east. Obitz was able to have his troops transported out of Stolpe (approximately twenty kilometers east of Schlawe) by train, however more than 100 men were killed or wounded in a Soviet air raid on the station and railway tracks. Among the wounded was *Waffen-Hauptsturmführer* Obitz. As ranking officer, *Waffen-Hauptsturmführer* Martin, who arrived from Josefstadt, assumed command of the approximately 400 remaining men.

Divided into three companies, the unit, also called *SS-Ersatz-Bataillon Martin*, initially occupied quarters in three villages north of Neustadt. The designation "*Ersatz-Bataillon*" (replacement battalion) was probably assigned because the men were no longer considered fit for combat and at best could be employed as a reserve. When Soviet tanks approached the quarters, the French withdrew without a fight southeast towards Gotenhafen with the rest of *VII. Panzer-Korps*.

On March 18, 1945, the main line of resistance already ran from Rewa (Putziger Wiek) southwest along the Sagorsch River, then passed in a semicircle north of Dirschau to Danzig Bay. Two days later the Martin

Battalion received orders to defend Gotenhafen. The French volunteers took over a third line of positions. The second line was manned by Latvian SS men and in the first were (ethnic) German troops of the *4. SS-Polizei-Panzer-Grenadier-Division*.

The French troops were under constant Soviet artillery fire until April 1, 1945. The enemy breached the first defense lines but were stopped temporarily before the positions held by the Martin Battalion. Soon afterwards, however, the French troops joined the evacuation by sea to Hela already under way. From there, the following day they set sail on a mail ship for Copenhagen. After arriving there on April 5, 1945, the remaining troops proceeded to Fredericia, and finally on April 10, to Neustrelitz, where the elements of the division were supposed to be reunited.

Waffen-Grenadier-Regiment der SS "Charlemagne" (französische Nr. 1)

After the division had been completely destroyed in its roughly three weeks of operations in Pomerania, as of March 16, 1945, the principal task for *SS-Brigadeführer* Krukenberg was to collect and reorganize the individual units coming across the Oder. The first assembly area was Jargelin and Menzlin northeast of Anklam. On March 24, 1945, the assembled French units moved into the Neustrelitz area. They numbered just about 1,100 men, however, to which were added another 250 members of the Martin Battalion. The rest, the French troops who had been in Kolberg, were dispatched to Wildflecken. In Pomerania, therefore, the division had lost more than 65% of its original strength—killed, severely wounded, captured or deserted.

By order of the *SS-Führungshauptamt* on March 25, 1945, the division was to be rested and reequipped with consent of Army Group Vistula:

1.) By order of the *RF-SS*, the *33. Waffen-Grenadier-Division der SS "Charlemagne"* (*franz. Nr. 1*) is to be rehabilitated at short notice in the area east of Neustrelitz.

2.) Organization: (I.D. 45 as guide)

1 *Gren. Rgt.* With 2 *Gren.* Battalions, 1 heavy battalion, consisting of:
1 anti-tank company,
1 tank-destroyer company,
1 flak company (1-2 batteries)

For the division command: 1 signals platoon, 1 pioneer platoon, 1 supply column,
1 workshop platoon

3.) The role of division headquarters will be assumed by the Inspectorate of French SS Units until further notice.

4.) Completion of rehabilitation: April 15, 1945

5.) The *SS-FHA* is responsible for the rehabilitation of the unit.

6.) Personnel Provisions:

a) Rehabilitation is to take place using all remnant elements of the division and incorporating all trained personnel of the French SS Grenadier Training and Replacement Battalion, Wildflecken.

b) To this end the French SS Grenadier Training and Replacement Battalion is to dispatch all trained personnel to the division by March 31, 1945.

Completion report by the *FS* to *SS-FHA*.

Transportation in agreement with *SS-FHA*, *TO-SS*.

The intended organization had little in common with an Infantry Division 45, however. The Army High Command had announced the new I.D. 45 organization on December 10, 1944. It envisaged the following authorized strength:

	352	officers
	29	civilian officials
	1,947	non-commissioned officers
	9,581	enlisted men (including 698 volunteer auxiliaries)
Total:	11,909	men

The division's materiel was to consist of:

7,594	rifles
1,563	pistols
462	light machine-guns
74	heavy machine-guns
79	mortars
10	37 mm anti-aircraft guns
11	75 mm anti-tank guns
35	infantry guns
25	105 mm light field howitzers
12	150 mm heavy field howitzers
14	assault guns
138	motorcycles
148	automobiles
185	trucks
32	*Raupenschlepper Ost* tractors
1,271	horse-drawn vehicles
368	other vehicles and
1,456	bicycles

The envisaged framework units were:

Division headquarters with map section and military police squad
3 grenadier regiments each with 1 regimental headquarters with headquarters company
  2 battalions each with 3 rifle companies and a heavy company
  infantry gun company
  tank destroyer company
Fusilier battalion with three rifle companies and a heavy company on bicycles
Anti-tank battalion with
  1st (Anti-Tank) Company with 12 75 mm self-propelled anti-tank guns
  2nd (Tank Destroyer) Company with 14 assault guns
  3rd (Flak) Company with 9 self-propelled 37 mm anti-aircraft guns
Artillery regiment with headquarters battery
3 battalions with headquarters battery and 2 batteries of 105 mm light field howitzers (horse-drawn) and 1 battery of 6 field guns
1 heavy battalion of 150 mm heavy field howitzers with headquarters battery and 2 batteries each with 6 guns (horse-drawn)
Pioneer battalion with 3 companies (partly motorized)
Signals battalion (abbreviated) with
  Field telephone company (partly motorized) and radio company (motorized)
Supply echelon
Field replacement battalion with 4 companies
Division combat school
Medical company (partly motorized)
Ambulance platoon
Division supply regiment with
  Division administration company (partly motorized) with
  Bakery and butchery platoon
  1 motor transport company
  2 bicycle troops
  1 supply platoon (partly motorized)
  1 workshop company (partly motorized)
Veterinary company (horse-drawn)
Field post office (partly motorized)

The *SS-Führungshauptamt* noted in its rehabilitation order that the division was to consist of a single regiment—ultimately designated ***Waffen-Grenadier-Regiment der SS "Charlemagne."*** The primary reason for this was to deceive the enemy. It was in fact a unit, which at that time consisted of only about 1,350 men, who were to be joined by another roughly 1,200 men from the replacement unit, designated the ***33. Waffen-Grenadier-Division der SS "Charlemagne."*** To what degree enemy intelligence was fooled is not known. It is, however, certain that it led to self-deception on the part of Hitler and Himmler. In the end they could no longer distinguish which troop strengths they actually still had. For example orders were issued to army corps that did not even have the fighting strength of a division.

After the *SS-Führungshauptamt* had ordered on March 18, 1945, that: "the personnel on hand in the French training and replacement battalion in *Wildflecken* [...] are to be transferred to the field replacement unit of the *33. Waffen-Grenadier-Division der SS "Charlemagne"(franz. Nr. 1)* after four weeks of basic training."[31] At the end of March 1945 it finally ordered the immediate transfer of the entire French SS Grenadier Training and Replacement Battalion into the refreshment area of the *33. Waffen-Grenadier-Division der SS "Charlemagne" (französische Nr. 1)* approximately 400 kilometers away. At the beginning of April 1945, therefore, about 1,200 Frenchmen left the training camp at Wildflecken, which was occupied by the Americans on April 7, on foot. Because of the rapid Allied advance, however, *SS-Obersturmbannführer* Hersche led his battalion to southern Germany, where it was ultimately captured by the Americans.[32]

The remaining elements of the "division" were assigned the following locations in the refreshment area:

Inspector of French Volunteer Units of the Waffen-SS	Carpin
Waffen-Grenadier-Regiment der SS "Charlemagne"	Grammerthin
I. Bataillon of former Regiment 57	Fürstensee
II. Bataillon of former Regiment 58	Wokuhl
III. (schweres) Bataillon	Goldenbaum
Division Combat School	Georgenhof
SS-Feldgendarmerie-Trupp 57 (military police)	Thurow
Motor Pool and Workshop Platoon	Zinow

In Neustrelitz, *SS-Brigadeführer* Krukenberg, inspector of French volunteer units of the Waffen-SS—who was acting as commanding officer—issued an order of the day that spoke of the catastrophic conditions:

> We have drastic days of bitter fighting and forced marches behind us. We have not fought as a small group within the German Army, but as an independent French division. With the name "Charlemagne" the French reputation for bravery and endurance has again been confirmed. The duration of our struggles has united us. [...]
>
> Everywhere we have helped hold back or stop the surging wave of bolshevism. This struggle could not be fought without serious losses and many of our comrades have not yet been able to make it back to our lines. We hope that General Puaud and with him other heroic fighters will soon be with us again. The struggle has welded us together. The fact that our division has been fused in glorious battles should be to our advantage, as we now form a block, a team.
>
> Far from our homeland, we can add new glory to our banner. We know that all Frenchmen, who like us stand for the freedom of the motherland and for the new European order, view us with pride. [...]
>
> The reputation of the LVF in the east, the success of the French SS Assault Brigade in the Carpathians, the battles fought by the militia in our motherland must create a block which, sealed by the French blood shed in Pomerania, must lead to the birth hour of a tradition that is worthy of the revolutionary idea for which we are fighting. Our belief in the victory of National Socialism is unshakeable. It will become even more determined if the situation becomes more difficult.
>
> At the side of our German comrades who are fighting for the same ideal, we follow the Führer, the liberator of Europe.

The rhetorical order of the day still had an effect on just a small part of the members of the "division," however. It did, however, show Krukenberg's national-socialist convictions, which he would soon express in several death sentences against French volunteers. These were in part imposed for various offenses for which the leaders of the affected units had imposed minor punishments but for which Dr. Krukenberg, a lawyer himself, had ordered new trials with the objective of the death penalty. For example, four Frenchmen who had been ordered to guard a Luftwaffe supply dump near Fürstensee had stolen, among other things, a large quantity of margarine. After *SS-Brigadeführer* and Doctor of Law Krukenberg found the sentence imposed by *Waffen-Sturmbannführer* Boudet-Gheusi too lenient, he ordered a new trial under *Waffen-Hauptsturmführer* Fenet. He immediately imposed the death sentence on all four men. The sentence was carried out the very next morning.

This was greeted with incomprehension by the men, and not only those who had one volunteered to serve alongside the Germans for pragmatic reasons. It also led those who had volunteered with enthusiasm to fight for National Socialism to feel that they were nothing more than "cannon fodder" for Germany. Instead of experiencing gratitude, comrades were now being shot "to maintain discipline" for "trifling offenses."

Conscious of this smoldering situation, *SS-Brigadeführer* Krukenberg freed the remaining Frenchmen to decide if they wanted to continue to serve in a construction battalion or a combat battalion. About 400 men subsequently volunteered for service in a construction battalion, which was formed in Drewin on April 10, 1945.

After the French SS Training and Replacement Battalion with its 1,200 members failed to reach the Neustrelitz refreshment area and met only the remnants of the Martin Battalion coming from Denmark, it was not possible to even realize the planned formation of a combat-capable regiment. All that existed were two weak battalions from the remnants of *Waffen-Grenadier-Regimenter der SS 57* and *58*, each with about 400 men, a mixed anti-tank company with about 150 soldiers and the unarmed construction battalion (mainly former members of the *Kriegsmarine* and the *Organisation Todt*). All of these units were attached to the commander of the *3. Armee*'s rear area used to construct anti-tank barricades in the area south and east of Neustrelitz.

Somewhat paradoxically, it seems that a *Generalmajor—SS-Oberführer* Puaud was still considered missing—was exercising command over about 1,350 men. This is suggested by the composition of a division headquarters, most of whose personnel came from the Inspectorate of French Volunteer Units of the Waffen-SS:

Commanding officer	*SS-Brigadeführer* Krukenberg
Headquarters commander	*SS-Obersturmführer* Ruhnow
1st Aide-de-Camp	*SS-Untersturmführer* Hegewald
Ia (1st General Staff Officer)	*SS-Hauptsturmführer* Pachur
Ib (2nd general Staff Officer)	*SS-Obersturmführer* Meier
Ic (3rd General Staff Officer)	*SS-Obersturmführer* von Wallenrodt
IIa/b (Personnel)	*SS-Hauptsturmführer* Pachur
IVa (administration)	*SS-Hauptsturmführer* Hagen
IVb (medical section)	*SS-Sturmbannführer* Dr. Schlegel
IVd (chaplain)	*Waffen-Untersturmführer* Abbé Verney
V (motor vehicle section)	*SS-Untersturmführer* Neubauer
VI (ideology)	*SS-Untersturmführer* Dr. Beuler
Military Police Squad	*SS-Obersturmführer* Görr
Division Combat School	*SS-Obersturmführer* Weber

With approximately 900 members, the *Waffen-Grenadier-Regiment der SS "Charlemagne" (franz. Nr. 1)* had about 50% of its authorized strength and its complement was thus equivalent to that of a reinforced battalion:

Commanding Officer	*SS-Standartenführer* Zimmermann

I. Bataillon (also referred to as *SS-Bataillon 57*)

Commander	*Waffen-Hauptsturmführer* Fenet
1st Company	*Waffen-Untersturmführer* Brazier
2nd Company	*Waffen-Obersturmführer* Bartoloméi
3rd Company	*Waffen-Untersturmführer* Counil
4th Company	*Waffen-Oberscharführer* Couvreur

II. Bataillon (also referred to as *SS-Bataillon 58*)

Commander	*SS-Hauptsturmführer* Jauss
5th Company	*Waffen-Oberscharführer* Hennecart
6th Company	*Waffen-Unterscharführer* Albert
7th Company	*Waffen-Standartenoberjunker* Million-Rousseau
8th Company	*Waffen-Untersturmführer* Colnion

III. (schweres) Bataillon (one anti-tank company)

Commander	*Waffen-Sturmbannführer* Boudet-Gheusi

Französisches Bau-Bataillon (French Construction Battalion)

Commander	*Waffen-Hauptsturmführer* Roy
1st Company	*Waffen-Obersturmführer* Roumgous
2nd Company	*Waffen-Obersturmführer* Gromini
3rd Company	*Waffen-Obersturmführer* Darrigade

Action in Berlin

During the night of April 24, 1945, *SS-Brigadeführer* Krukenberg received two telephone calls at his headquarters, a farmhouse in Carpin. The first came from the SS Personnel Office, informing him that he was to take command of a division in Berlin, and the second was from the *3. Panzer-Armee*, ordering him to immediately make his way to Berlin with a battalion and report to the Reich Chancellery.

The battalion was to bolster Berlin's defenses until the *12. Armee* under *General* Wenck relieved the Reich capital from the Potsdam area. Because of Krukenberg's assessment that the French SS volunteers still offered the greatest reliability, the *I. Bataillon* (*Waffen-Hauptsturmführer* Fenet) and the Division Combat School (*SS-Obersturmführer* Weber) were selected to go to Berlin.

Transporting more than 600 men to Berlin, about 150 kilometers away, presented problems, however. Rail transport was no longer possible, and of the forty-four trucks the division had before its deployment to Pomerania, at least on paper, only about six were serviceable. As well, there was little fuel available for any of its vehicles.

In the end, only about 120 men could be loaded into four light trucks, one of which broke down on the way.[33] Thus, in the end, the convoy consisted of three trucks and two cars, in which were *SS-Brigadeführer* Krukenberg, *SS-Hauptsturmführer* Pachur and *SS-Untersturmführer* Patzak, plus *Waffen-Hauptsturmführer* Fenet with *SS-Obersturmführer* Weber and *Waffen-Untersturmführer* Michel.

The column left Carpin early on April 24, 1945, and initially proceeded to Alt-Strelitz. From there it drove via Neuruppin–Löwenburg to Nauen. When the men arrived in Falkenrehde at about 1500, members of the *Volkssturm* mistook them for a Soviet advance force and blew the bridge across the Havel. The just under 100 men were forced to clamber over the remains of the bridge with their equipment and continue on foot towards Berlin. Following the Army Road, at about 2200 they arrived at Olympia Station.

There *SS-Brigadeführer* Krukenberg gave his men permission to open a nearby, unguarded air force supply depot and help themselves to various things. This is noteworthy, because less than four weeks earlier four Frenchmen had been shot for the very same action on Doctor of Law Krukenberg's express order!

At about midnight, as ordered, Dr. Krukenberg arrived in the Reich Chancellery, where he received orders to report to *General der Artillerie* Weidling, commander of the Berlin Defense Area,[34] the next morning. Weidling gave him command of the remnants of the *11. Freiwilligen-Panzer-Grenadier-Division "Nordland." SS-Brigadeführer* Ziegler, the division's former commander, who was much loved by his men, had shown reluctance to see his division sacrificed in the hopeless battle for Berlin and was transferred to the officer reserve. It was hoped that in *SS-Brigadeführer* Krukenberg they had a commander who followed orders without hesitation. Krukenberg remembered:[35]

> *General* Weidling told me that the southeast part of the city, Defense Sector C, was entrusted to the *11. Freiwilligen-Panzer-Grenadier-Division "Nordland,"* which was part of his panzer corps. Apparently, however, its commanding officer was no longer holding his unit together. He had encountered members of the division wandering about aimlessly in various parts of West Berlin. After a heated argument about this, he had seen himself forced to request the removal of division commander *SS-Brigadeführer* Ziegler, who otherwise had been an excellent officer.

While the Red Army closed the ring around Berlin near Ketzin on April 25, 1945, trucks collected the roughly ninety French SS volunteers from Olympia Station and delivered them with *SS-Brigadeführer* Krukenberg to the *11. Freiwilligen-Panzer-Grenadier-Division "Nordland"* command post in Neukölln in the Hasenheide. Then *SS-Unterscharführer* Burgkart (battalion operations officer/*SS-Division Nordland*) recalled the relief of his division commander by *SS-Brigadeführer* Krukenberg:

> On the morning of April 25, 1945, we—*SS-Sturmbannführer* Saalbach, *SS-Sturmbannführer* Vollmar and I—were standing and talking in front of the stairs to the forward command post—a building of the sanatorium in the Hasenheide. Suddenly someone addressed us from behind: "Where is the *Nordland* command post?" I turned around and said: "Down there in the cellar." And as I said it I saw the silver-grey greatcoat flaps and that it was an *SS-Brigadeführer*. He was standing behind me, somewhat to my right, at the corner of the house. Without saying a word he walked past us—followed by several SS men with assault rifles under their arms.

The area of operations in Neukölln between the town hall and Richard Square.

When I looked around, I saw that a few trucks carrying SS people had driven up without our notice. The men had got out and had sealed off the entire road in a form of skirmish line. Everyone was stopped. We were still standing, completely surprised, in front of the cellar entrance, when a few minutes later *SS-Brigadeführer* Ziegler came up the stairs with his driver, *SS-Hauptsturmführer* Emmert and his batman. Ziegler came straight towards me and said: "Burgkart, take your mess kit from the car and any other private things you might have."

I asked: "Why *Brigadeführer*?" The answer: "Remove your things, I have to go now!"

Only then did I learn that the second *SS-Brigadeführer* was Dr. Krukenberg of the *33. Waffen-Grenadier-Division der SS "Charlemagne"* and that the SS men with him were French.

By then, Emmert had already climbed into the *Schwimmwagen* and had started its engine. I removed my case, my assault rifle and my jacket. Then Ziegler and his batman got in. He stood in the front of the car, saluted us and said to the two *SS-Sturmbannführer* standing next to us: "Good luck gentlemen!"

When he was gone, *SS-Sturmbannführer* Vollmar looked at me and said: "What's going on?" And then again: "What's going on?" I disappeared for a few moments to take care of a few things and when I tried to return to the command post I was stopped by one of the Frenchmen: "No, back! No, back!"

"Man, who wants to go back!" I screamed. At that moment, when neither understood the other correctly, two or three armored troop carriers carrying wounded SS men approached. They had come from the area south of Hasenheide. The crews were looking for a hospital for their groaning, wailing and screaming comrades. "Halt, stop, stop," the Frenchman shouted again. The drivers ignored him and kept going. Suddenly one of the Frenchmen raised his assault rifle and fired at the leading troop carrier. The co-driver behind the MG-42 reacted by simply firing into the French SS men. I saw three or four Frenchmen rolling on the ground and screaming. Now, I thought to myself, get out of here as quickly as possible. With the rest of the operations staff I drove to the new command post in the state opera house on the Unter den Linden. There we were divided into squads and deployed at Spittelmarkt Square.

After the handover of command, which obviously took place in an extremely cool and tense atmosphere, the French SS volunteers formed a so-called assault company with about nine squads. Three squads formed platoons, which were commanded by the officers present (Fenet, Wallenrodt and Weber). They thus acted as platoon leaders. The guiding principle behind assault units is described in the study *The Infantry Battalion and the Assault Battalion Developed in the Waffen-SS during the War*:[36]

> The assault squad was equipped with assault rifles, rifles with telescopic sights, light machine-guns, rifle grenade equipment and hand grenades. *Panzerfaust* anti-tank weapons were added later. The next largest unit, the assault platoon, also had mortars as heavier high-angle weapons. As well, the assault company had heavy machine-guns, mortars, often 20 mm cannon, anti-tank rifles and infantry pioneers with demolition and mining equipment.
>
> The style of warfare waged by such a unit was typified by assault teams or squads receiving their own combat assignments which they, committed next to each other, carried out in close combat if possible, while leaving certain gaps and exploiting existing terrain conditions.

For the Frenchmen of the *Sturm-Kompanie* (assault company) this meant separate actions in the ruins of houses in Berlin. On the morning of April 26, 1945, they moved to the town hall of Neukölln and there took part in an attack towards the south to Richard–Platz with elements of the *11. Freiwilligen-Panzer-Grenadier-Division "Nordland"*—which still numbered about 1,500 fighting men. In the street and house fighting the men were finally forced back towards the town hall. The enemy quickly infiltrated the surrounding houses and contact with the German units was lost, resulting in the decision to pull the troops back towards the Hermannplatz. Also there were armored units, which were capable of offering greater resistance.

Finally an order arrived from *LVI. Panzer-Korps* for the *SS-Division "Nordland"* to move to Defense Sector Z (*Zentrum* = center). This sector was under the command of *SS-Brigadeführer* Mohnke and was divided into two sub-sectors. One, called West, was under *Oberstleutnant* Seifert, whose headquarters were in the State Ministry of Aviation (RLM), and the other, designated East, extended along Leipziger Strasse in front of the RLM to Döhnhoffplatz, was assigned to *SS-Brigadeführer* Krukenberg. He moved into his new command post in the *Stadtmitte* (city center) underground station on April 27, 1945.

Above: The State Ministry of Aviation; below: the new Reich Chancellery.

The French volunteers were ordered to Hedemannstrasse, where they reinforced elements of the *SS-Freiwilligen-Panzer Grenadier Regiment 24 "Danmark"* deployed there. Their main role there was combating enemy tanks, shooting at advancing Soviet tanks from the windows and cellars of wrecked houses with panzerfausts. On April 28–29, 1945, the men were in the ruins of Wilhelm- and Puttkamer-Strasse, trying to take out Soviet tanks that made repeated advances from the direction of Belle Alliance Square.

On March 7, 1945, Hitler had ordered that any soldier who destroyed six enemy tanks with close-range weapons should be awarded the Knight's Cross of the Iron Cross in addition to the Special Badge for Single-Handed Tank Destruction,[37] introduced in 1942. French *SS-Unterscharführer* Vaulot was so decorated on April 29, 1945. After the war *SS-Brigadeführer* Krukenberg remembered: [38]

> The combating of Russian support tanks by our assault guns, but in particular by the French tank-destroyer squads, played a significant role in the defense. After knocking out two T-34s with *panzerfausts* in Neukölln, French *Unterscharführer* Vaulot destroyed six more enemy tanks in a similar fashion within twenty-four hours. On my recommendation he was subsequently awarded the Knight's Cross of the Iron Cross. I was able to present it to him on the afternoon of April 29, in the presence of my staff and his assembled French comrades by candlelight in my command post in the underground tunnel. In a speech given in French, I declared that the personal actions of this young volunteer befitted the historical reputation that the soldiers of France had earned through their bravery on all the battlefields of the world. *Sturmbannführer* Herzig, commander of *SS-Panzer-Abteilung 503*, was also awarded the Knight's Cross that day and received it from the hand of *Brigadeführer* Mohnke.
>
> Worthy of mention in addition to outstanding individual actions by members of *Nordland*, are those of French volunteers *Hauptsturmführer* Fenet and *Standarten-Junker* Apollot, likewise the fact that German *Obersturmführer* Weber, a member of my staff, was awarded the Special Badge for Single-Handed Tank Destruction in Gold for destroying his fifth enemy tank on one of the last days of the war.

It has been claimed that the Knight's Cross of the Iron Cross was also awarded to former *Waffen-Hauptsturmführer* Fenet, *Waffen-Standarten-Junker* Apollot and *SS-Obersturmführer* Weber. The decorations were allegedly awarded by

SS-Brigadeführer Mohnke, however, this cannot be confirmed. In any case the award applications should have been made by *SS-Brigadeführer* Krukenberg, who was in direct command of the French troops. The Knight's Cross could not be awarded by either Mohnke or Krukenberg directly, as such awards followed the usual chain of command until Hitler's death. This meant that an award application was submitted by the division and approved by the next-highest command (in this case the *LVI. Panzer-Korps*), and had to be submitted to the Army Personnel Office. After a positive preliminary decision the application was passed on to the OKW/Adjutancy and finally to Hitler for a decision. With Hitler's death, the authority to award the Knight's Cross passed to *Großadmiral* Dönitz. On the question of the awarding of these three Knight's Crosses and the fundamental strength of the French volunteers who fought in Berlin—which is usually given in the literature as 400 to 500—Dr. Krukenberg remembered:[38]

> There were ninety volunteers under *Hauptsturmführer* Henri Fenet. The French speak of approximately 500 (?), on the basis of which documents I do not know. Fenet and an *Untersturmführer* Apollot also claim that they have the Knight's Cross. They point to the German *Obersturmführer* Weber. I know nothing, however, about any of the three receiving the Knight's Cross! In my opinion it is an invention![39]

Yielding to superior Soviet forces, on April 30, 1945, those who had survived the inferno of the final battle in Berlin fell back towards Prinz-Albrecht-Strasse around the State Ministry of Aviation. Farther north, at 1425, two Red Army soldiers ran up the first Soviet flag from a window of the German Reichstag and at 2200 raised the flag on the dome of the building. In the area of the Ministry of Aviation, meanwhile, on May 1, 1945, there was an atmosphere of hysteria. A member of the *11. Freiwilligen-Panzer-Grenadier-Division "Nordland"* remembered:

> On April 28, 1945, we received orders to take up position in the Prussian State Printing Office. The next day Russian tanks came without pause from the direction of the Hallesche Tor. Russian infantry tried to break through using flamethrowers and explosive charges. At about 2200 on April 30, 1945, we decided to retreat to the State Ministry of Aviation. There was chaos there—no one knew what was happening. During the night of May 1, 1945, we found the train in the Friedrichsstrasse. As everything was in

> the hysteria of dissolution, we three comrades also split up. While the others went to the aid stations, I, as a Berliner, went home.

After the suicides of Hitler and other leading Nazis, *General der Infanterie* Krebs, chief of the army general staff, initiated surrender negotiations with the Soviets, whereupon *General der Artillerie* Weidling ordered the troops under his command to prepare to break out. The men were supposed to make their way in small groups in the general direction of Neuruppin. At about 2200 hours on May 1, 1945, *SS-Brigadeführer* Krukenberg dispatched runners to advise the troops under his command that at 2300 they should leave the main line of resistance and assemble at Friedrichsstrasse Station in preparation for the breakout. While Weber's platoon together with elements of the *11. Freiwilligen-Panzer-Grenadier-Division "Nordland"*—supported by the remaining armored vehicles—launched the breakout across the Weidendammer Bridge, the Fenet Platoon was obviously not advised of the impending breakout attempt. The group under Krukenberg, which had been joined by former division commander *SS-Brigadeführer* Ziegler, marched towards Invalidenstrasse. Powerful enemy forces caused the soldiers to turn east towards Brunnenstrasse and from there they tried to reach Humboldt-Hain. As Soviet troops were also everywhere there, they were taken prisoner one after another.

Waffen-Hauptsturmführer Fenet and the remaining thirty Frenchmen, on the other hand, tried to make their way to the *12. Armee*. Following the underground network, the men headed southwest. Fenet later remembered:

> The Russians attacked with the utmost ferocity through the whole night and the entire morning of May 1. The situation grew worse on the afternoon of May 1. Our building partly collapsed and long wooden beams hung down to the street from the ground floor. A wonderful target for the flamethrowers of the Russians, who, exploiting our weakness, were infiltrating the ruins everywhere. In vain we tried to throw the beams down onto the street. After several attempts the Russians succeeded in setting fire to the wood. We didn't have a drop of water with which to put out the fire.
>
> On the morning of May 2, we pulled back to the aviation ministry and made contact with the Luftwaffe units holding onto the building. We wasted no time preparing to join the defense there, but no sooner

were we ready when vehicles bearing white flags approached from the enemy lines. Sitting in them were German and Russian officers. There was talk of surrender and in fact soon afterwards unarmed Russian soldiers came and offered us cigarettes.

But we couldn't believe that everything was supposed to be over. That was impossible! In any case we couldn't simply give up. What was happening in the Reich Chancellery? We would at least be able to find out something there, and if a final block of resistance was to be formed, then we would form it there.

We quickly left the ministry. Avoiding the streets, we made our way through the ruins to the underground, climbing down into the tunnel through an airshaft. We walked to the Kaiserhof underground station, which was right behind the Reich Chancellery. An iron ladder led up to the grate that was placed over the airshaft. I was first to climb up. After the climb I expected to hear sounds of fighting. What reached my ear, however, was the wild sound of automobile horns and rolling trucks. Several more rungs and I could see. As my fingers clutched the ladder, my eyes beheld an incomprehensible spectacle. In the Wilhelmplatz, as far as one could see, were Russians and vehicles with the red star. Not a single shot was fired at them. The walls of the Reich Chancellery were silent. There was no one left, it was all over!

We had to get out of there. In my opinion there was only one solution. We had to try to break through to the west. We would use the underground tunnels as long as possible. Forwards—we would do it this time too. A bitter disappointment awaited us at the Potsdamer Platz. From there the underground line continued in the open air.

The best thing now was to hide underground and wait for night. We quickly split up into small groups and disappeared one after another. At that moment we were approached by Volkssturm men who had the same intention as we. These poor elderly men were less mobile and attracted the attention of Russian soldiers, who passed by soon afterwards. "Don't shoot, don't shoot," cried the first of them in a fearful voice. The soldiers searched the entire area carefully and our groups were ferreted out one after another.

At the same time, *General* Weidling's order to cease fighting, prepared by the Soviets, was announced by loudspeaker:

> The *Führer* committed suicide on April 30, 1945, abandoning all those who swore loyalty to him. True to the Führer's order, you, German soldiers, were ready to continue the struggle for Berlin, even though you were running out of ammunition and the overall situation made further resistance futile. I order the immediate cessation of all resistance. Every hour that we continue fighting prolongs the awful suffering of the civilian population of Berlin and our wounded. In agreement with the senior commanders of the Soviet forces, I also call upon you to immediately cease hostilities.

The Battle of Berlin was over. Precise casualty figures for the week-long battle are not available. It is estimated, however, that about 6,000 German soldiers and *Volkssturm* members were killed in the street fighting in the Reich capital, including about thirty-five French SS volunteers.

Then *SS-Untersturmführer* Emil Zwingert was a member of SS Battle Group Mohnke. He described the last three days of fighting in Berlin and also recalled the French SS volunteers:

> A summons by the army commander of Berlin obliged all members of the armed forces in Berlin to report immediately to the Seeckt Barracks. On the way there—public transport was no longer operating—I was stopped by a Waffen-SS *Kübelwagen* in Belle Alliance Square.
>
> The officers were members of Battle Group Mohnke and among them was *SS-Untersturmführer* Bauer, with whom I had been in *SS-Panzerjäger-Ersatz-Abteilung 1* in Rastenburg and at the anti-tank school in Prague. I didn't know if they were out "hero snatching," however we then drove together to the old Reich bank, where we took charge of two brand-new 50 mm anti-tank guns. One group of six to eight men was assigned to serve the guns. We moved one gun into position on Leipziger Strasse—just in front of the *Spittelmarkt*—with orders to keep the Russian tanks out. As we had no armor-piercing ammunition, we had to fire high-explosive shells with delay fuses. Behind us in the Bärenstiefelhaus was a group of Charlemagne men, who were constantly coming and going with *panzerfausts*. We stood with our backs to the wall, submachine-guns cocked, and waited for the Russians to appear. Then we struck out for the assembly point at the Friedrichsstrasse underground station. We made it, passing rubble, debris, ruins and many dead—many committed suicide. All the while Russian shells fell among the waiting crowds of

people (soldiers and civilians). The breakout attempts were probably doomed from the start.

The guns fell silent in Berlin on May 2, 1945. Wandering through the ruined city, I suddenly ran into the Russians. They were not particularly watchful and I was able to get away. Civilians offered me clothes. People cautiously emerged from their cellars onto the street. While creeping in the direction of Tempelhof, I was arrested beneath the overhead railway in Kreuzberg because I was wearing military boots under my civilian trousers.

The End in Mecklenburg–Western Pomerania

After *SS-Brigadeführer* Krukenberg and his ninety volunteers left the Neustrelitz rehabilitation area for Berlin on April 24, 1945, *SS-Standartenführer* Zimmermann was left in command of the approximately 1,200 remaining French troops. Initially they continued building positions in front of the rehabilitation area.

On April 28, in the course of their offensive that had begun on April 20, 1945, about ninety kilometers farther east in the Schillersdorf–Kolbitzow–Hohenzahden area, the first Soviet armored units reached the line Ueckermünde–Fürstenwerder–Feldberg–Lychen–Templin. This placed the enemy spearheads only about thirty kilometers from Neustrelitz. The remnants of the *33. Waffen-Grenadier-Division der SS "Charlemagne"* were subsequently attached to *XXXXVI. Panzer-Korps* (*General der Panzertruppen* Gareis) and took over the defense of tank barriers near Carpin (approximately fifteen kilometers east of Neustrelitz) and Fürstensee (approximately seven kilometers south of Neustrelitz). After *SS-Standartenführer* Zimmermann was hospitalized due to an injury, *Waffen-Sturmbannführer* Boudet-Gheusi assumed command of the men for the last four days.

The French Construction Battalion under the command of *Waffen-Hauptsturmführer* Roy had already moved to the northwest via Waren on April 27, 1945, in order to reach the demarcation line in the area north of Schwerin Lake. The fighting troops followed two days later, after turning their defensive duties in the rear area over to units of the Wehrmacht. After assembling in Neustrelitz they initially marched towards Wesenberg (approximately twelve kilometers southwest of Neustrelitz) and then turned north.

Beginning on April 30, 1945, the *Waffen-Grenadier-Division der SS "Charlemagne"* was placed under the tactical command of the *XXXII. Armee-Korps* (*General der Infanterie* Schack) and tried in all haste, together with fleeing civilians and retreating Wehrmacht units, to reach the demarcation line near Bad Kleinen (approximately twelve kilometers south of Wismar), which was about 100 kilometers away, by way of Waren and Güstrow.

The regiment was disbanded there by *Waffen-Sturmbannführer* Boudet-Gheusi on May 2, 1945. He advised the French volunteers to pass themselves off as former prisoners of war who had been working in German agriculture.

The German core personnel were either to join other German units in becoming prisoners of war or try to disappear among the civilian population. For those who were taken prisoner by the Soviets—like those in Berlin, for example—this as a rule resulted in a sentence of twenty years in a labor camp. The men were, however, released by 1956. Most of those who ended up in French custody after the war also received prison sentences. Charles de Gaulle, however, permitted members of the former *33. Waffen-Grenadier-Division der SS "Charlemagne"* to rehabilitate themselves in the Foreign Legion. Not long afterwards their path led to Indo-China.[42]

The *Französische Ausbildungs-u. Ersatz-Bataillon der SS*[43]

By order of the *SS-Führungshauptamt* of August 26, 1944, the Training and Replacement Detachment of the French Legion (LVF) in Greifenberg was merged with the French Training and Cadre Company of the French SS Volunteer Assault Brigade. The new unit was initially called the French SS Grenadier Training and Replacement Battalion. Its envisaged organization was as follows:

1 battalion headquarters with mortar training section
4 rifle training companies
1 driver training section
1 cadre company
1 convalescent company

SS-Sturmbannführer Tramu, former battalion commander in the LVF, was named commander of the new battalion (station: Greifenberg, Pomerania) and accepted the responsibilities transferred to him. These were:

a.) Assemble training companies from recruits with the same induction dates.
b.) Form trained replacement companies only as required, if recruit training was completed and orders for action at the front have not yet been issued.
c.) Ensure that placement, issuing of uniforms and creation of all personnel documents (e.g. pay books, military I.D. cards) are all carried out in the cadre company and that it also looks after already-trained personnel.
d.) Assign all convalescents released from hospital to the convalescent company, provided they require further medical treatment.

In the first ten days of October 1944, the last French recruits under the command of *SS-Obersturmbannführer* Hersche were transferred from the SS training camp in Sennheim to the replacement unit in Pomerania, which had since been renamed *Französisches Ausbildungs- und Ersatz-Bataillon der SS* (French SS Training and Replacement Battalion). Effective October 13, 1944, the former *I. Bataillon*/SS Training Camp Sennheim was deemed disbanded—thus ending the unusual secondment of a military unit to the *SS-Hauptamt*. On November 28, *SS-Obersturmbannführer* Hersche took over from *SS-Obersturmbannführer* Tramu as commander of the now approximately 1,800-man-strong battalion. Its organization at that time was as follows:

Commanding Officer	*SS-Obersturmbannführer* Hersche
Adjutant	*SS-Hauptsturmführer* Kroepsch
Abt. III	*SS-Obersturmführer* Dick
Abt. VI	*SS-Obersturmführer* Dr. Zander
Cadre Company (825 men)	*SS-Untersturmführer* Kipp
Training Company (430 men)	*Waffen-Obersturmführer* Crespin
1st Company (180 men)	*SS-Obersturmführer* Ludwig
2nd Company (180 men)	*Waffen-Obersturmführer* Michel
3rd Company(180 men)	*SS-Obersturmführer* Allgeier

As had happened in the brigade in October 1944, the training and replacement unit now also underwent a check of the men's reliability. In this process about 250 Frenchmen were dismissed from the unit as "undesirable."

Subsequent training in the now about 1,550-men-strong French SS Training and Replacement Battalion can only be described as improvised. The overall situation resulted in a loss of motivation—and not just in this battalion. The onset of winter made things even worse. Despite inadequate winter clothing and poor rations, an attempt was made to enhance infantry training, especially the use of close-range weapons against tanks.

On January 23, 1945, *SS-Feldersatz-Bataillon* was formed from the over-strength cadre company, which consisted mainly of soldiers who had recovered from wounds, under the command of *SS-Hauptsturmführer* Biziau, and at the end of February 1945, it was sent to Körlin to join the *33. SS Waffen-Grenadier-Division der SS "Charlemagne"* that was at the front.

About five weeks later—just before the Red Army reached Greifenberg at the beginning of March 1945—first the civilian population and then the approximately 900 men of the French SS Grenadier Training and Replacement

Battalion were evacuated. The soldiers were moved to the Wildflecken training camp. While seventeen-year-old German troops with just four weeks of training were being sent to the front in Pomerania, the French battalion was obviously not regarded as a fighting unit despite at least three months of training.

Barely three weeks later the *Reichsführer-SS* changed his mind, however, and on March 18, 1945 the *SS-Führungshauptamt*[44] ordered:

> After four weeks of basic training, the men in the French SS Training and Replacement Battalion are to be transferred to the field replacement unit of the *33. SS Waffen-Grenadier-Division der SS "Charlemagne" (franz. Nr. 1).*

At the end of March the *SS-Führungshauptamt* ultimately ordered—not least because of the rapid advance by American forces—that the French SS Grenadier Training and Replacement Battalion be sent to the *33. SS Waffen-Grenadier-Division der SS "Charlemagne"* (franz. Nr. 1)'s rehabilitation area in Neustrelitz. The replacement unit had thus spent less than four weeks at the Wildflecken troop training camp and now had been sent to almost the exact place from where it had been transferred to Wildflecken.

During the night of March 31, 1945, almost 1,000 French troops left Wildflecken on foot. The 900 men from Greifenberg had been joined by a number of convalescents from the hospitals and the odd volunteer. *SS-Obersturmbannführer* Hersche used these men to form two groups. One was an armed trained replacement battalion (*SS-Sturmbannführer* Katzian) and a lightly armed Special Battalion (*Sonder-Bataillon*) under *SS-Sturmbannführer* von Lölhöffel. The latter unit was made up in part of Frenchmen who had been court-martialled.

The first march destination was Meiningen, about forty kilometers to the northeast. There, *SS-Obersturmbannführer* Hersche received a new directive for him and his troops to withdraw south towards the so-called Alpine Redoubt. The soldiers marched via Sonneberg and Kronach to Marktredwitz, from where they were transported by rail to Regensburg.

On the evening of April 14, 1945, the two groups marched out of Regensburg. Some elements made night foot marches in the direction of Pfaffenhofen and from there via Freising to Traunstein and Bad Reichenhall.

There was no enemy contact. Other elements marched to Landshut where, on April 29, 1945, they were attached to the *38. SS-Grenadier-Division "Nibelungen,"* part of the *XIII. SS-Armee-Korps*, along the Isar River.

These French companies subsequently occupied positions near Moosburg against the advancing Americans and after the first contacts with the enemy, on May 2, 1945, they were pulled back towards Wasserburg am Inn. From there, still attached to the *38. SS-Grenadier-Division "Nibelungen,"* they moved along the Chiemsee in the direction of Bad Reichenhall. When American troops occupied the town on May 4, 1945, elements of the French SS Grenadier Training and Replacement Battalion were taken prisoner. Other elements made it as far as Lofer, where they, too, were captured.

When it was made known that the French SS volunteers were going to be handed over to the approaching French 2nd Armored Division (Gen. Leclerc), twelve Frenchmen fled out of fear of reprisals. Recaptured, on May 8, 1945, they were shot by order of Gen. Leclerc. The reason for this was allegedly a "cheeky" reply by an SS volunteer. Asked by Leclerc why he was wearing a German uniform, the prisoner asked back why the general was wearing an American uniform and not a French one.

Precise details are not known, but to Gen. Leclerc the French eastern front volunteers were simply collaborators and traitors. The shooting of prisoners of war, which of course was contrary to military law, was not an isolated case. When captured (this time by the Wehrmacht or Waffen-SS), German soldiers, former prisoners of war or deserters who acted against Germany on the Soviet side as members of the National Committee for a Free Germany, were usually treated no differently.

Conclusion

The story of the French units in the "struggle against Communism" was marked by a certain skepticism towards them by the German side. The formation of a division was not desired at first, and the French Volunteer Legion (LVF) formed by the army only saw action before Moscow for about a week in December 1941. Afterwards it was used exclusively for anti-partisan duties to secure the rear areas. This was also no simple task, but as a rule units were used which were less than fully qualified for use at the front or were of questionable reliability in the eyes of the Wehrmacht.

Surprisingly, the French units of the Waffen-SS were not in front-line service much longer. *I./Französische SS-Freiwilligen-Sturmbrigade* was only in the main line of resistance in Galicia between August 12–15, 1944, and from the twentieth to twenty-fourth of the same month. After these nine days, the next front-line action, by the *33. SS Waffen Grenadier Division der SS "Charlemagne,"* was not until half a year later, from February 23 to about March 16, 1945, in Pomerania. The last and best-known action after these roughly three weeks, was for ninety French volunteers, the final battle in Berlin, which once again lasted barely a week. French SS volunteers had thus been in action for a maximum of about five weeks during the entire time of their existence. André Bayle, who had been one of the first French SS volunteers in March 1943, and who almost exactly two years later—on March 8, 1945—was captured by the Poles in Pomerania, had precisely twenty-two days of front-line service during his two years in the Waffen-SS.

In this respect, it is also interesting to see how the men reflected on their service in the Waffen-SS after the war. As described in the foreword, there are many publications on this topic, however, most are lacking in historical objectivity. Such perspectives are surely not representative of all French volunteers, who suffered extremely heavy casualties during their brief actions, but veterans with common ideals did get together after the war. Quantitatively representing less than 5% of the former members of the *33. SS Waffen Grenadier Division der SS "Charlemagne,"* they still, or perhaps directly because of their position in postwar society, felt themselves animated by the "thought of a National-Socialist Europe." They saw themselves as the elite of France and so a former French SS volunteer wrote to the editors of *Der*

Ausweg (*The Way Out*)—the newsletter of HIAG (the Mutual Aid Organization of Members of the former Waffen-SS)[45] six years after the end of the war:

> Dear comrades!
>
> My warmest thanks for sending *The Way Out*.
>
> For me and for several friends, it has been a very pleasant surprise to discover the unbreakable bonds that were created by our shared actions at the front.
>
> Reading your (or should I say instead: our) newsletter brought to life in us many moving memories. The years of defamation of the German soldier and especially of SS members (which for us is far from ended), seems to have come to an end in Germany. So may it be for us someday.
>
> It seems to me completely superfluous to once again stress what we wanted back then—the victory of a strong Europe over the bolshevist threat. That Germany was in the lead had nothing to do with this deep necessity. Once there was a European army (about which so much is blathered today) and we were it. Cursed in our homeland as traitors and criminals, we feel closely tied to you German comrades.
>
> Even though just 6,000 Frenchmen fell in the east, it is nevertheless proof that there existed a higher imperative than chauvinistic nationalism in the fateful hours of World War Two. We loved France and Germany, but the Waffen-SS was our shared Fatherland and all of Europe its territory. For that reason the events of the war cannot be forgotten. We all heard Europe's fateful hour striking; who can deny it now. All who once swore the oath of loyalty to the black flag with hand raised remain bound to it until death and can never forget that sacred moment. Dear comrades, please forgive my spelling mistakes. I would be happy if I could make clear what my local comrades and I myself feel, even if somewhat clumsily.
>
> We are of course not permitted to form an association in which we can meet every year and most of us are still under police surveillance, and for obvious reasons we are not free to become members in any German association. The main thing is, however, that the principle of mutual aid exists here too and that with it material difficulties or other hardships can be eased.

For many, this attitude remained unchanged with the passage of years, as shown by a meeting of former SS volunteers on the provisional fiftieth anniversary of the establishment of the French SS Volunteer Regiment on

March 7, 1993. The widow of *Waffen-Oberführer* Puaud, commanding officer of the *33. Waffen-Grenadier-Division SS "Charlemagne,"* sent the following explicit words of greeting:

> Dear friends,
>
> I do not know all of you, and yet you are often in my thoughts; so too on this 7th of March, which almost coincides with the date of my husband's death. As you know, that was on the morning of March 6, 1945 in Belgard cemetery in Pomerania.
>
> How I would like to be with you today, to better express the gratitude I feel for that which was your commanding officer's and my purpose in life. I am certain that your reunion will only strengthen the spirit of comradeship that always animated you and which he always wished for.
>
> I therefore allow myself to ask you in his name to stick together like brothers. You all showed the same courage, no matter if it was in the LVF, the militia or the SS Assault Brigade.
>
> Your choice was the right one, but you all know the saying, which is still true: one is always in the wrong when one is too soon right.
>
> Be proud that you were first to want to break free from old ideologies, for which we are persecuted with hate and feelings of revenge; but there is no doubt. Soon they will have to vacate the field.
>
> I am with you with all my heart and ask that you accept my wish that your reunions continue for a long time.
>
> With the expression of my very great sympathy,
>
> Signed, J. Puaud.

Another twenty years have since gone by, and despite various political and economic difficulties there is no talk of abandoning democracy. Just as seventy years ago, ideas such as these have shown themselves to be representative neither of France nor Germany.

Appendices

The French Vichy Government

After the defeat of the French armies in the summer of 1940, the former President Lebrun gave Marshall Pétain the task of forming a new government and conducting the imminent cease-fire negotiations with Germany. The cease-fire was ultimately signed at Compiègne on June 22, 1940. As a result of the treaty, France was divided into an occupied zone under German military administration and an unoccupied part in the south of the country. The so-called Vichy government (*Régime de Vichy*) set itself up there with Marshal Pétain as president (*Chef de l'État*) and Pierre Laval as Pime Minister.[46]

Although Pétain declared France's neutrality, Vichy France supported Germany economically, militarily and politically. Even though, as we see in this book, military cooperation was not significant, France was Germany's most important trading partner during the Second World War and it achieved almost full employment of its people. In addition to producing military equipment for the Wehrmacht in its own country, almost a million Frenchmen also worked in Germany. The French prime minister passed a law stating that mandatory labor service also had to be carried out abroad—meaning Germany. After nearly 250,000 Frenchmen voluntarily went to work in Germany after an initial recruiting phase, following a second German request for another 250,000 French workers mandatory labor service (*Service du travail obligatoire*) was introduced to achieve this figure. A third action followed in August 1943, in which another 100,000 workers were gathered and the beginning of 1944 a fourth brought another 50,000 French workers. In the end, volunteers made up only a small percentage.

The Vichy government's policies towards the Jews were repugnant. Within a few weeks in 1940, the first measures resulted in foreign Jews being excluded from society and one year later general discrimination against Jews living in France. Deportations to concentration and death camps in the *Generalgouvernement* (Poland) began in the summer of 1942. Both the French police and the militia took part in the rounding up of the Jews.

After the Allies landed in North Africa in November 1942, German troops occupied the south of France. This step, which supposed to prevent an invasion on the south coast of France, had no influence on the Vichy government, however, which continued to represent governmental power. This did not end until August 20, 1944, when the government under Pétain[47] was evacuated to Sigmaringen. On August 25, 1944, the provisional government of the Republic of France (*Gouvernement provisoire de la République Français*) under the leadership of Charles de Gaulle took over the running of the country.

The French Volunteer Legion (LVF)

After the start of "Operation Barbarossa," there arose a desire among the rightist movements in France to send volunteers to take part in the struggle against bolshevism. Hitler rejected the formation of a 30,000-man-strong division, but did authorize a regiment-size unit. Marshall Pétain subsequently approved the voluntary joining of a legion in occupied and unoccupied France.

The "*Légion des Volontaires Français contre le Bolchvisme*" (LVF) was founded soon afterwards on August 5, 1941. Recruiting for the legion was undertaken by the Central Committee of the French Volunteer Legion under its president Eugéne Deloncle, whose recruiting office was in Marseille. A first contingent of twenty-five officers and 803 other ranks—all trained soldiers—moved into the Borgnis-Desbordes barracks in Marseille on August 27, 1941. On September 5, 1941, the men were transferred to Demba training camp (*Generalgouvernement*). The legion was formed there under the command of Col. Labonne. The second contingent of 127 officers and 769 other ranks arrived there on September 20, 1941. A third contingent with twenty-one officers, 125 noncommissioned officers and 498 enlisted men reached the former Polish troop training camp on October 12, 1941.

From these 2,352 volunteers, formation of *Französische Infanterie-Regiment 638* (French Infantry Regiment 638) began:

Regimental Headquarters	Military Postal Code 00 100
Headquarters Company	Military Postal Code 00 100
I. Bataillon	Military Postal Code 03 865
German liaison staff	Military Postal Code 39 630
II. Bataillon	Military Postal Code 04 358
German Liaison Staff	Military Postal Code 56 381
III. Bataillon	Military Postal Code 19 440
13th (Infantry Gun) Company	Military Postal Code 01 196
14th (Anti-Tank) Company	Military Postal Code 02 732
15th (Motorcycle) Company	Military Postal Code 47 702
French Artillery Battalion	Military Postal Code 06 376
Replacement and Training Detachment	Military Postal Code 46 795

The idea that the French volunteers might march into Moscow with the Germans in December 1941 was not realized.

From the spring of 1942 the LVF was used solely in the anti-partisan role, taking part in many large "counter-bandit operations."

At the end of October 1941, the regimental headquarters plus the first and second battalions were transported by rail to Smolensk and on November 19, 1941, they were attached to the 7th Infantry Division. Four more troop contingents from France arrived in Demba between December 1, 1941, and February 19, 1942, and were used to form the *III. Bataillon* and the Replacement and Training Detachment.

The *I* and *II Batallions* went into action before Moscow on December 1–3, 1941, and were ordered to take the town of Dyukovo. The units failed in their task, and after many volunteers fell victim to frostbite the units were withdrawn from action on December 6–8, 1941.

The LVF was not a homogenous unit as its members had been recruited from many right-wing organizations. As a result, quarrels among its members were common. In April 1942, the OKH forbade any political activity in the regiment and surprisingly gave the volunteers permission to leave army service if they so desired.

Most members of the *Movement Social Révolutionaire* (led by Deloncle) took advantage of this offer, as a result of which the strength of the battalions was reduced almost by half. The battalions had, however, been overstrength, consequently they were still at authorized strength. Politically, the *Parti Populaire Française*, whose leader Doriot had himself volunteered for the LVF, now provided the bulk of the volunteers in French Infantry Regiment 638.

While the *I* and *II Battalions* had already been assigned to anti-partisan duties in Army Group Center's rear area, usually separate from one another, on May 10, 1942, the *III. Bataillon* moved from Demba to the Potshinok area (approximately 60 km southwest of Smolensk) where it was attached to the *221. Sicherungs-Division* (221st Security Division). Because of casualties, the *II. Bataillon* was temporarily disbanded in the summer of 1942 and its remaining men assigned to the other two battalions. The *I. Bataillon* was subsequently also referred to as the "Radom Battalion" and the *III. Bataillon* as the "Demba Battalion."

Among the actions in which the units took part were:

17/05/42	*III. Bataillon* operated as part of the 221st Security Division against partisans in the Baltutino area.
04/06 – 08/06/42	*II.* and *III. Bataillon* in the valley of Volost, taking Pavlova and Galashino.
06/07 – 28/08/42	Both battalions took part in "Operation Greif" in the area astride the Orsha–Vitebsk road (under Senior SS and Police Commander Russia Center)
08/42	*I. Bataillon* took part in "Operation See" in the Smolensk area.
29/08 – 28/11/42	*III. Bataillon* in action securing the Belynkovichi–Krichev–Orsha rail line in the area north of the Beresino–Cherven road. *I. Bataillon* attached to the 286th Security Division and *III. Bataillon* again to the 221st Security Division.
Beginning of 1943	*I. Bataillon* employed in the Smorki area.
28/01/43	*III. Bataillon* in action under the *2. Panzer-Armee* in the Mamayevka Forest.
02/43	*I. Bataillon* still attached to Grenadier Regiment 931 (286th Security Division) and *III. Bataillon* to Luftwaffe Field Training Regiment 36 (221st Security Division).
05/43	I. Bataillon in combat in the Kotovo area.

10/05 – 25/07/43 *III. Bataillon* in action guarding the Mogilev–Byalynichi and Mogilev–Cechevhi communications roads. Secured the area between the line BorisovTolochin in the north, the Tolochin–Mogilev road in the east and the Beresina to Murovo in the west.

10/43 The French Artillery Battalion was disbanded and its personnel distributed among the grenadier battalions. The formation of a *IV. Bataillon* from artillerymen did not take place.

Battalion in action west of Mogilev.

11/43 Regiment in action in the Shepelevichi area.

02/44 "Operation Marocco" in Beresina – Pogost area. Forty-one partisan villages and 1,000 blockhouses destroyed. 1,181 partisans killed and 1,346 captured. Col. Puaud was awarded the Iron Cross, Second Class for his actions.

25/05 – 17/06/44 *III. Bataillon* in "Operation Kormoran" in the Polotsk area.

23/06/44 Start of retreat by *4. Armee* from the Palik area towards the Beresina with objective of Borisov. *I. Bataillon* and two companies from the *III. Bataillon* secured bridgehead over the Bobr (approx. 50 km east of Borisov). Held the important bridgehead position together with *SS-Polizei-Regiment 2* until July 27, 1944, destroying approximately forty Soviet tanks in the process.

10/07/44 Order from Army Group Center to Headquarters, *4. Armee* for the remnants of French Grenadier Regiment 638 to be sent to Greifenberg, Pomerania. Assembled in Camp Moritz south of Minsk, after which the westward withdrawal by the French began.

Brief Biographies

Edgar Puaud

Edgar Puaud was born in Orléans on October 29, 1889, and joined the military in 1909. Sgt. Puaud was made an officer candidate on August 5, 1914, and ended the First World War as a captain. Initially assigned to the Army of the Rhine, he subsequently saw action in Morocco from 1926 to 1937. There he was a battalion commander in the French Foreign Legion. Back in France, he commanded the III Battalion of the 23rd Infantry Regiment. In July 1942, Puaud joined the newly formed *Legion Tricolore* and there was appointed colonel on November 25, 1942.[48] After the legion was disbanded on December 28, 1942, Col. Puaud volunteered for the LVF. On February 20, 1944, he was awarded the Iron Cross, Second Class. At the end of August he had discussions with Himmler about merging the LVF and the French SS Volunteer Assault Brigade. Puaud was named *Waffen-Oberführer* on September 1, 1944, and awarded the Iron Cross, First Class. At the same time he was given command of the new *Waffen-Grenadier-Brigade der SS "Charlemagne" (französisch Nr. 1)*. Surprisingly, Puaud was responsible for a not inconsiderable number of volunteers being sent to concentration or labor camps. His main reason for doing this was an attempt to create the most effective brigade possible. The volunteers of the LVF had not been scrutinized as closely (for previous offenses and political attitudes) as was done in the Waffen-SS. Wounded and physically exhausted, *Waffen-Oberführer* Puaud probably took his own life in Belgard cemetery on March 6, 1945.

Henri Fènét

Henri Fènét was born in Ceyzeriat (Ain) on June 2, 1919, and studied literature at the *Faculte des Lettres* in Paris. He ended his studies prematurely in September 1939 to join the military. He was promoted to lieutenant in 1940 and on November 29, 1942, joined the French Militia. In October 1943, Fènét volunteered for the Waffen-SS and was taken in as an *SS-Standartenoberjunker*. After the conclusion of the "1st Course for French Officers at the Tölz SS Officer School" he was promoted to *SS-Untersturmführer*. He served as a company commander in the French SS Volunteer Assault Brigade and was awarded the Iron Cross, Second Class on August 22, 1944. When the *Waffen-Grenadier-Brigade der SS "Charlemagne"* was formed, he commanded *I./Waffen-Grenadier Regiment der SS 57* as a *Waffen-Obersturmführer*. During the retreat from Pomerania, he succeeded in leading his battalion west without serious loss. For this he received the Iron Cross, First Class from the commanding general of Korps Munzel and on March 18, 1945, he was promoted to *Waffen-Hauptsturmführer*. His last action took him to Berlin, where he was captured by the Soviets. He was personally brave and tactically gifted, however, the death sentences he handed down to French volunteers cast a shadow over him, and although his destruction of Soviet tanks met the conditions for the awarding of the Knight's Cross, he did not receive this prestigious decoration by war's end. He died in Paris on September 14, 2002.

Dr. Jur. Gustav Krukenberg

Gustav Krukenberg was born in Bonn on March 8, 1888, and in 1907, joined the Prussian Army as a *Fähnrich*. He studied and graduated in legal science and during the First World War his service included positions as aide-de-camp and adjutant. In 1918, he completed a general staff officer course in Sedan and was promoted to *Hauptmann* in Headquarters, *LVIII. Armee-Korps*. From the end of the war until 1920 he worked in the ceasefire committee in Versailles. In 1926 he took over the German-French Study Committee in Paris. Back in Germany, Krukenberg became advisor to the State Commissioner of Broadcasting and soon afterwards took over the commissioner's position himself. He joined the NSDAP in 1932 (membership number 1,067,635), and the SS on May 30, 1933 (membership number 116,686). Released from state radio because of differences with Dr. Goebbels, he headed a chemical company in Berlin until the end of 1939. In 1940, he was reactivated with the rank of *Major der Reserve* (in the SS he had been an *SS-Obersturmbannführer* since January 30, 1938). Deployed in the Netherlands, and from 1941 Paris, in 1943 he was transferred to the staff of the Economic Inspectorate Center in White Russia. There Dr. Krukenberg's duties included the "procurement" of so-called foreign workers for the German economy. At the age of fifty-five he again volunteered for active service and joined the Waffen-SS. On December 1, 1943, he was assigned to *SS-Panzergrenadier-Ausbildungs- und Ersatz-Bataillon 1* as an *SS-Obersturmbannführer der Reserve*. On January 17, 1944, he was assigned to the *V. SS-Freiwilligen-Gebirgs-Korps* in the Balkans as chief-of-staff and soon afterwards was promoted to *SS-Standartenführer*. Just a few weeks later he and other staff members were relieved for "unsuitable behavior." The unsuitable behavior was probably similar to that which led to the removal of *SS-Brigadeführer* von Oberkamp, commander of the *7. SS-Freiwilligen-Gebirgs-Division "Prinz Eugen"*: arrogant disinterest in the ethnic German and Bosnian corps members. Surprisingly, however, Krukenberg's career continued on an upwards path and on May 9, 1944, he was promoted to *SS-Oberführer* and named chief-of-staff of the *VI. SS-Freiwilligen-Armeekorps (lettisches)*. There, too, however, his position was a brief one. After the disastrous command of the Latvian volunteers on the eastern front, he and the completely overburdened commanding general *SS-Gruppenführer* von Treuenfeld were relieved on July 25, 1944. This was followed by a brief four-week stint as commander of the Waffen-SS "Ostland," and on August 26, 1944, he was placed in charge of the German liaison staff attached to the French SS Brigade, which later became the Inspectorate of

French Volunteer Units of the Waffen-SS. During operations in Pomerania, Krukenberg took over division command from *Waffen-Oberführer* Puaud. Finally, for a few days before the end of the war he was placed in command of the *11. SS-Freiwilligen-Panzer-Grenadier-Division Nordland* and on May 12, 1945, he was captured by the Soviets. Initially imprisoned in Bautzen and later in Brandenburg, he surprisingly escaped the fate of being deported to the USSR. Krukenberg was released in April 1956, and he finally died at the age of ninety-two in 1996.

Rank Comparisons

The following table compares ranks of the French Army, the Heer, and the Waffen-SS:

French	Heer	Waffen-SS
Soldat 2nd Class	*Schütze*	*Schütze*
Soldat 1st Class	*Oberschütze*	*Oberschütze*
Caporal	*Gefreiter*	*Sturmmann*
Caporal-Chef	*Obergefreiter*	*Rottenführer*
Sergent	*Unteroffizier*	*Unterscharführer*
Elève-officier Sergent	*Fahnenjunker*	*Junker*
Sergent-Chef	*Unterfeldwebel*	*Scharführer*
Elève-officier Adjudant	*Fähnrich*	*Standartenjunker*
Adjudant	*Feldwebel*	*Oberscharführer*
Adjudant-Chef	*Oberfeldwebel*	*Hauptscharführer*
Adjudant-Chef de Cie	*Kompanie-Feldwebel*	*Stabsscharführer*
Aspirant	*Oberfähnrich*	*Standartenoberjunker*
Sous-Lieutenant	*Leutnant*	*Untersturmführer*
Lieutenant	*Oberleutnant*	*Obersturmführer*
Capitaine	*Hauptmann*	*Hauptsturmführer*
Commandant	*Major*	*Sturmbannführer*
Lieutenant-Colonel	*Oberstleutnant*	*Obersturmbannführer*
Colonel	*Oberst*	*Standartenführer*
—	—	*Oberführer*
Général de Brigade	*Generalmajor*	*Brigadeführer*
Général de Division	*Generalleutnant*	*Gruppenführer*
Général de Corps d´Armée	*General*	*Obergruppenführer*
Général d´Armée	*Generaloberst*	*Oberst-Gruppenführer*

Endnotes

1. In particular the Netherlands, Denmark, Norway and Sweden.

2. Volunteers who were not fully up to SS standards or men who, while they wished to fight against communism, had no desire to serve in the Waffen-SS, were taken into volunteer legions. Organizationally, however, they were subordinate to the *SS-Führungshauptamt*.

3. Michael Wildt, et al., *Der Dienstkalender Heinrich Himmlers 1941/42* (Hamburg, 1999) 633.

4. Ibid., 641.

5. Ibid., 58.

6. See Werner Haas, *Europa soll Leben!* (Berlin, 1936).

7. André Bayle recalled the name of the office where he volunteered in March 1943 incorrectly, however. Its proper name from spring 1943 until September 26, 1943, was "Recruiting Center for French Volunteers for the Waffen-SS." Only later, until May 18, 1944, was the office in Paris called the "Replacement Command for Waffen-SS France." It was subsequently relocated and from December 20, 1944, to January 30, 1945, was called "SS Replacement Command France."

8. Interestingly, there were frequent contacts between the French volunteers and the Wallonian Rexist leader Leon Degrelle. On January 31, 1943, for example, he gave an "inspiring" speech at the Berlin Sports Palace before several thousand Wallonian and French armaments workers. On March 5, 1944, following the first action on the eastern front by the SS Volunteer Assault Brigade "Wallonien" (in the Cherkassy Pocket), he gave an appeal in the Palais Chaillot in Paris. The goal of this was to recruit French volunteers for the Waffen-SS. One year later, after learning of the dispute between the militia, the LVF and the Waffen-SS, he proposed that the French Militia be incorporated into his unit. After talks with Degrelle in 1945, *SS-Obergruppenführer* Karl-Hermann Frank, senior SS and police commander for Bohemia and Moravia, considered him "the" political leader for Wallonian and French collaborationist movements.

9. The SS Troop Training Camp Sennheim was under the *SS-Hauptamt* and was set up in Alsace in 1940. It was a collection and training camp for Germanic SS volunteers who, on the one hand, were to be examined for suitability, and on the other given preparation for actual military training—in particular through sports and language instruction (commands and orders in the German language). The Swiss *SS-Sturmbannführer* Hersche became commander of the *I. (französische) Bataillon/SS-Ausbildungslager Sennheim* (I [French] Battalion/SS Training Camp Sennheim).

10. The following military postal codes were assigned on March 13, 1944:

HQ and HQ Battery	11 003	I Battalion	13 847
II Battalion	12 175	III Battalion	14 049
Artillery Train	13 847	Observation Battery	06 386

11. See: Vicennz Oertle, *Ein Appenzeller in der Waffen-SS* (Appenzell, 2012).

12. Hersche was simultaneously promoted to *SS-Obersturmbannführer*.

13. A cliché typically used by SS officers in referring to foreign volunteers. Himmler said something similar in August 1944 in conversations with Bronislav Kaminski, the former commander of the Russian "RONA" *Volkswehr* Brigade. On that occasion he declared that—in reference to the attempt on Hitler's life on July 20, 1944—he would prefer to have a bodyguard of Russian volunteers.

14. Just three grenadier companies are given in some of the literature. As the battalion's strength was about 1,000 men, however, it can be assumed that there were in fact four grenadier companies. A total of six companies (including the HQ Company and the 5th Anti-Tank Company) with a strength of about 160 men per company results in a total of 960 troops, to which must be added the battalion headquarters.

15. Quoted from: "Wiking-Ruf," Year 4, April 1955, No.4.

16. To the north of it was the large Heidelager SS training camp.

17. SS-FHA, Amt II Org. Abt. Ia/II, Diary No.2710/44 secret command matter of 26 August 1944.

18. *SS-Hauptamt*, Diary No.106/44 secret command matter of February 8, 1944.

19. The designation as regiments with the consecutive Waffen-SS numbers 57 and 58 did not take place until late 1944. Although the brigade was not officially called the 57th *SS Waffen Grenadier Brigade "Charlemagne,"* its other units were given the number 57.

20. Also see the chapter, "The French SS Grenadier Training and Replacement Battalion."

21. At that time Darnand was serving as a *Freiwilligen-Hauptsturmführer* in the 28th SS Volunteer Grenadier Division "*Wallonien*" (Wallonian No. 1).

22. See Rolf Michaelis, *Die SS-Heimwehr Danzig im Polenfeldzug* (Eggolsheim, 2011).

23. In some cases they simply perished, were taken prisoner or succeeded in finding their way to a larger unit or section of the front.

24. Telex OKH/GenStdH/Op Abt (Roman I a), No.450 037/45 secret matter for the commander.

25. Center against Expulsions: report by Dr. Hans Leeser, the former mayor of the city of Elbing in West Prussia, of 29 May 1952.

26. Albert Forster was born in Fürth (Central Franconia) on July 26, 1902, and attended a classical grammar school. He later worked as a bank clerk before going into politics. He was given various positions in the NSDAP, including Gauleiter of West Prussia. His comment about the *Reichsführer-SS*—"if I looked like Himmler, I wouldn't talk about race!"—is interesting. Forster was hanged in Poland on February 28, 1952.

27. Headquarters, Army Group Vistula, *Reichsführer-SS* Himmler, Abt. I a, Diary No.139/45 secret command matter of January 30, 1945.

28. André Beaurivage may be in error here and it was in fact Neustettin Station.

29. See chapter, "Action in Kolberg."

30. See "Conclusion."

31. The *Reichsführer-SS*, field headquarters, March 18, 1945, diary no. 3040/45 secret.

32. See chapter "French SS Grenadier Training and Replacement Battalion."

33. The publications that state that approximately 500 French volunteers were transferred to Berlin claim that 45–50 men or even entire companies were transported in one truck. As the division had only light trucks, such as the Opel Blitz, this could not be achieved, even if the men stood.

34. *General der Artillerie* Weidling, commanding general of the *LVI. Panzer-Korps*, had been tasked with the defense of Berlin.

35. Dr. Gustav Krukenberg, *Kampftage in Berlin* (Bonn, 1958).

36. Kurt Gropp, *Das Infanterie-Bataillon und das in der Waffen-SS während des Krieges entwicklte Sturm-Bataillon* (*The Infantry Battalion and the Assault Battalion Developed in the Waffen-SS During the War*) (Historical Division Headquarters United States Army, Europe, no year).

37. See Rolf Michaelis, *Das Sonderabzeichen für das Niederkämpfen von Panzerkampfwagen durch Einzelkämpfer* (Berlin, 2010).

38. Dr. Gustav Krukenberg, *Kampftage in Berlin* (Bonn, 1958).

39. Dr. Gustav Krukenberg, *Kampftage in Berlin* (Bonn, 1958).

40. As the immediate superior, Dr. Krukenberg would had to have made an application for the awarding of the Knight's Cross. As well there is no proof in the award files of the OKW that the decorations were awarded. It can therefore be assumed that these three Knight's Crosses were to a certain extent "wishful thinking." Veit Scherzer, author of the book *Die Ritterkreuzträger*, told me that he included the three soldiers in his book based on statements made after the war. This recollection by Dr. Krukenberg, which excludes this, was unknown to him.

41. Henri Fenet, *Die letzte Runde – Franzosen kämpfen um Berlin* (no location, no date).

42. See: ZDFHistory.de

43. See Vincenz Oertle, *Ein Appenzeller in der Waffen-SS* (Appenzell, 2012).

44. The *Reichsführer-SS*, field headquarters, March 18, 1945, No. 3040/45 secret.

45. Quoted from "Der Ausweg," Issue 7, December 1951.

46. Admiral François Darlan was prime minister from February 1941 to April 1942.

47. After the war Pétain and other members of the Vichy government returned to France and were charged by the provisional government with high treason and collaboration. Pétain was given the death penalty on August 15, 1945, however, this was commuted to life in prison. He died there in 1951.

48. The *Legion Tricolore* can be seen as the forerunner of the later Militia under Joseph Darnand, and on October 5, 1942, it had fifty-four officers, 118 noncommissioned officers, and 595 enlisted men. When the legion was disbanded in December 1942, the bulk of the battalion-strength force joined the militia. About 100 legionnaires volunteer to serve in French Infantry Regiment 638 on the eastern front. They included officers Bassompierre, Boudet-Gheusi, and Obiz, who were later battalion commanders in the LVF and Waffen-SS.

Bibliography

Bayle, André. *Von Marseille bis Nowosibirsk*. Rosenheim, 1994.

Fenet, Henri. *Die letzte Runde – Franzosen kämpfen um Berlin*. Publisher unknown, nd.

Forbes, Robert. *For Europe*. Solihull, 2006.

Gropp, Kurt. *Das Infanterie-Bataillon und das in der Waffen-SS während des Krieges entwickelte Sturm-Bataillon*. Historical Headquarters, United States Army, Europe, nd.

Haas, Werner. *Europa will leben!* Berlin, 1936.

Kruckenberg, Dr. Gustav. *Kampftage in Berlin*. Bonn, 1958.

Longerich, Peter. *Heinrich Himmler*. Berlin, 2010,

Mabire, Jean. *Berlin im Todeskampf 1945*. Preußisch Oldendorf, 1977.

—. *La Brigade Frankreich*. Paris, 1973

—. *La Division Charlemagne*. Paris, 1974

Michaelis, Rolf. *Die Waffen-SS: Mythos und Wirklichkeit*. Berlin, 2006.

—. *Das Sonderabzeichen für das Niederkämpfen von Panzerkampfwagen durch Einzelkämpfer*. Berlin, 2010.

Oertle, Vincenz. *Ein Appenzeller in der Waffen-SS*. Appenzeil, 2012.

Schöttler, Peter. "Dreierlei Kollaboration: Europa-Konzepte und deutsch-französische Verständigung – am Biespiel der Karriere von SS-Brigadeführer Gustav Kruckenberg." *Zeithistosche Foeschungen/ Studies in Contemporary History*, Online-Ausgabe, September 2012.

Soulat, Robert. *Geschichte der Division "Charlemagne."* Publisher unknown, nd.

Wildt, Michael. *Der Dienstkalender Heinrich Himmler 1941–42.* Hamburg, 1999.